M000119838

BREATH
OF
LIFE

DANIEL KOOMAN

FOREWORD BY SIGMUND BROUWER
Author of *The Last Disciple*

For my daughter Rosie,
While I held you in my arms
I saw the face of God.

The Breath of Life: Three Breaths That Shaped Humanity
Copyright © 2020 by Daniel Kooman

Red Arrow Media, LLC.
California.

All rights reserved.

No part of this publication may be reproduced, distributed, or transmitted in any form or by any means, including photocopying, recording, or other electronic or mechanical methods, without the prior written permission of the publisher, except in the case of brief quotations embodied in critical reviews and certain other noncommercial uses permitted by copyright law.

FIRST EDITION

All Scripture references marked (KJV) are taken from the Authorized King James Version. Public domain. All Scripture references marked (NKJV) are taken from the New King James Version®. Copyright © 1982 by Thomas Nelson. Used by permission. All rights reserved. All Scripture references marked (NET) are taken from NET Bible® copyright ©1996-2017 All rights reserved. Build 30170414 by Biblical Studies Press, L.L.C. Scripture and/or notes quoted by permission. All Scripture references marked (NIV) are taken from THE HOLY BIBLE, NEW INTERNATIONAL VERSION®, NIV® Copyright © 1973, 1978, 1984, 2011 by Biblica, Inc.® Used by permission. All rights reserved worldwide. All Scripture references marked (ISV) are taken from The Holy Bible: International Standard Version. Release 2.0, Build 2015.02.09. Copyright © 1995-2014 by ISV Foundation. ALL RIGHTS RESERVED INTERNATIONALLY. Used by permission of Davidson Press, LLC. All Scripture references marked (NLT) are taken from Holy Bible, New Living Translation, copyright © 1996, 2004, 2015 by Tyndale House Foundation. Used by permission of Tyndale House Publishers, Inc., Carol Stream, Illinois 60188. All rights reserved. All Scripture references marked (HCSB) are taken from Holman Christian Standard Bible® Copyright © 1999, 2000, 2002, 2003, 2009 by Holman Bible Publishers. Used with permission by Holman Bible Publishers, Nashville, Tennessee. All rights reserved. All Scripture references marked (LEB) are taken from the Lexham English Bible. Copyright 2012 Logos Bible Software. Lexham is a registered trademark of Logos Bible Software. All Scripture references marked (EHV) are taken from the Holy Bible, Evangelical Heritage Version® (EHV®) © 2019 Wartburg Project, Inc. All rights reserved. Used by permission. All Scripture references marked (ESV) are taken from the ESV® Bible (The Holy Bible, English Standard Version®). ESV® Text Edition: 2016. Copyright © 2001 by Crossway, a publishing ministry of Good News Publishers. The ESV® text has been reproduced in cooperation with and by permission of Good News Publishers. Unauwide. All Scripture references marked (WEB) are taken from the World English Bible®. Public Domain. All Scripture references marked (WNT) are taken from the Weymouth New Testament in Modern Speech Third Edition 1913. Public Domain.

ISBN: 978-0-578-85486-1

Cover Artwork: Mindi Oaten
Cover Design: Graeme Ellis
Interior: Vision Tank, UK

CONTENTS

FOREWORD

by Sigmund Brouwer
Author of *The Last Disciple, The Weeping Chamber*

Stories come from the words we hear that we choose to mine and treasure. In time, the words that we ponder over, and take time to cultivate, have a way of becoming flesh. As Daniel shares in *The Breath of Life*, this book is the story that unfolded after God whispered a simple, powerful word to him, "Breath."

Daniel and I both grew up in the small town of Red Deer, Alberta. A small dot on the very large map of Canada. Both Daniel and I trace our European heritage from Dutch immigrants that came to Canada following World War II.

Recently, Daniel reminded me that the first time we met was in the early 1990's, when I visited his Grade 4 class to share about my work as an author. Now an accomplished filmmaker and storyteller by trade, Daniel explained how that visit was the first time he ever thought about the significance of the written word, and by extension, the significance of the stories that we tell.

In its simplest form, the message I shared with Daniel and his Grade 4 class 25 years ago is that words have power, and the best words become the stories we tell, and the best stories have the power to change people. This book is a full circle reminder of that truth. In *The Breath of Life*, Daniel reminds us that The Word became flesh. He unpacks revelations from the Hebrew language, buried deep in the fabric of the Scriptures, that when mined from their roots become treasures that have been waiting in plain sight to be discovered.

I was most impacted by the deep revelation this book unveils around breath, which reminds us how quintessential the moment truly was when Yahweh breathed on Adam in the Garden of Eden. Breath changes everything. When Adam began to breathe, humanity began to bear God's image. To bear the image of God is to have a living soul, breathed or gifted to you by a living God. As you continue to breathe, your very existence remains tied to the Creator of breath. You are a living soul made in God's image. Is there a more powerful truth than this to ponder for ourselves? While many of us have read the Genesis creation story, and many of the important Scriptures about God's plan and promises, this book does something new in unveiling the purposes and love of God.

What Daniel shares about the Hebrew word "Ruach" left a deep imprint on my heart. The spirit and breath of God are an ever-moving, earth-shaping, universe-creating power. But also a mystery that resides in every believer. It's natural for us to think we are small, and we are in scale, within the vast universe. But if the power that raised Jesus from the dead lives in us, that is a wonder worth revisiting and understanding further so that we can know the full significance it brings to our own lives. In this book, Daniel also explains and reveals the original names of Father God, Jesus and The Holy Spirit, unpacking important revelations in the process. We are able to understand why Their names are not only important, but also the foundation humanity is built upon. What a powerful mystery, and reminder God has given us, once we have an understanding of His Name.

Reading this book, I was most surprised by the many meaningful layers of truth that Daniel was able to uncover. Truth that many of the original authors and translators of the Scripture left hovering below the surface of the written word. Here they are explained in a fresh and powerful way that applies to our daily lives.

I believe that in the current state of our world this book provides a timely relevance for readers. Daniel reminds us that there are two different spirits at work in the air that we breathe every day. As we discern that the Spirit of God is different than the spirit of this age, we begin to live in new areas of freedom, health, joy and passion. If every living soul needs breath to live, then each and every one of us will enjoy a fresh, new, holy breath of life!

In the same way that I never saw or expected to hear how seeds I never knew I was planting grow to fruition, I foresee that the power of Daniel's thoughts and stories shared in this book will have a wonderful impact in the lives of readers.

Sigmund Brouwer (December 30, 2020)

INTRODUCTION

A WORD ABOUT BREATH

The thing about breathing is it's automatic. The rhythm of human breath is automated by a network of neurons and muscles surrounding the lungs and throat. But how did this automation begin?

In February 2019 I discovered three breaths from the lungs of God that were breathed upon humanity and shaped the history of mankind. These breaths from God ultimately revealed to me one of the greatest mysteries I had ever uncovered and understood from my own personal studies in the Bible.

It began before an annual mission trip to Tanzania, when I asked the Lord for a word that would capture the purpose of our mission. What I received was quite literally one word. But that single word changed my relationship with God. The word was *Breath*. The unfolding of this journey continues to enlarge my faith and increase my unfading hope in the Creator of everything. This book is about the most epic truth you can ever discover and the story of my journey into this new revelation. I guess when He said, "Breath," Yahweh knew what He was talking about.

CHAPTER 1

RUACH ELOHIM - THE SPIRIT OF GOD

"In the beginning God created the heavens and the earth. Now the earth was formless and empty, darkness was over the surface of the deep, and the Spirit of God was hovering over the waters."

— Genesis 1:1–2 NIV

Imagine you are in a vast, dimly lit chamber. Through the darkness you make out the faint outline of a massive painter's canvas, completely blank. You walk toward it with a strong desire to create. Dense fog envelopes you until you reach the canvas. As you think about your need for paint and supplies, dozens of fresh paint colours appear beside you; a light, fine-tip paintbrush is now in your hand. It feels right to you, and you know exactly how to use it.

The mood would be better with music. You begin to hear the strings and swells from a full orchestra filling the chamber. The acoustics are fantastic in here. Now you feel charged and even more creative as the sound in the space and new melodies sweep over you. Your hand reaches effortlessly toward the first paint color, dipping into a glossy yellow as your mouth takes over, "Let there be light."

A sun forms on the canvas. The darkness of that place is separated by the piercing warm light of the sun. The pace of the music gains intensity, and your creativity flows all the more effortlessly. The paintbrush is no longer in your hand, but it still paints the canvas all the same so long as you continue speaking. Your words become substance the moment they leave your mouth, coming to life on the painting, and the words themselves multiply into creative expressions all their own.

"Let dry ground appear." Suddenly, sand becomes beaches, and beaches make way for rocks, and rocks turn into mountains. Looking at the once blank canvas, you begin to smile because what you see is so beautiful. And it is good. The canvas begins to fill from one corner to the other.

As you exhale with a sigh of deep satisfaction, a star comes out of your mouth and, moving into orbit, becomes indescribably massive. Planets and moons and entire galaxies begin to explode onto the canvas, and as they do, the canvas itself begins to expand and become multidimensional. The chamber you are standing in now begins to fill up with birds, creatures of all kinds, and wild animals innumerable.

Our first introduction to the God of all creation and mankind is as Spirit hovering over a vast ocean, looking at a blank canvas. While the earth is without form and void of life, we find our Creator in the preparation phase, undaunted, like a painter ready to begin a masterpiece. But before a stroke of paint hits the canvas, there is a period of brooding, of planning and preparation. In Genesis 1:2, we are introduced to this Spirit. In the original language, the Spirit of God translates into English as Ruach Elohim (*ruach* is pronounced "roo-awk").

As you unpack the original language used by the author of Genesis, layers of meaning begin to add depth to the narrative. For example, the word *hovering* describes Ruach Elohim as being in a state of soft relaxation while gently dancing over the face of the deep. The Spirit of God is described to be in a restful state. It's almost as if the longer Ruach Elohim waits, the more the energy builds, waiting for that explosive moment when creation itself will respond to God's voice. From this place of restful relaxation, the Spirit of God is hovering with immense energy and *getting ready to breathe.*

Ruach Elohim is also described as the Giver of Breath, Giver of Spirits. A Hebrew scholar explains the meaning of Ruach Elohim's name this way: "He is the breath of God which disperses His life-force, His energy and His intentions, His mind. Ruach Elohim is Yahweh's Spirit. Yahweh's breath."[1]

When God whispered, "Breath," to me before an annual mission to Tanzania, Africa, in 2019, a deep desire grew within me to understand the word and its context in Genesis 1 more clearly. To have a deeper understanding of *breath* in Scripture, I needed to know the original Hebrew wording and translation better, which meant diving into the language and reading the biblical text with the English beside the Hebrew.[2] Over the course of several months of study, I was stunned by the new layers of meaning and wordplay, but most of all, I was taken deeper into the realm of God's creativity as the story came alive like never before.

The first thing I found is that *breath* in Scripture is directly connected to the word or meaning for "spirit." That's because when the Hebrew word *ruach* is used, it means both "spirit" and "breath." But it means much more than that. Hebrew is a very colourful language that has characters or pictures that represent each word, adding layers of meaning on top of layers of revelation. As the English saying goes, "a picture is worth a thousand words." In this case that is especially true, since *ruach* is not simply spirit or breath in their essence, but rather the power encountered *within* the spirit or breath. Therefore, in the beginning of Genesis, *ruach* is not only spirit and breath, it is also the essence of the Almighty, pointing to Ruach Elohim as **God who is Spirit and the Giver of Breath.**

From His position of restful, hovering creativity, Ruach Elohim begins to create a perfect order.

"And it was very good."

And so, Ruach Elohim arrays the heavens and earth with splendor. Ruach Elohim begins to speak into existence immensely complex creativity, from which

---

1 Wikibooks, s.v. "Hebrew Roots/Trinity/Holy Spirit," last modified 15 March 2020, https://en.wikibooks.org/wiki/Hebrew_Roots/Trinity/Holy_Spirit

2 Today we have access to transliterations and interlinear versions of the Bible online, and Hebrew or Greek versions of the text are usually listed side by side with English versions in a number of our common English translations. The scholarship and effort making this available are a gift that can be accessed freely with a few clicks on Bible Hub or other websites and used during your own studies as well (See biblehub.com/interlinear for more information).

all of physics, science, and mathematics find their root. Here is an example from God's creation that still gives me goose bumps every time I think about it.[3]

The magnificent Hubble space telescope provided the image shown above.

Amber Straughn, an astrophysicist, explained that recently Hubble had been pointing for days into what they called "an empty black patch of nothingness."[4] It was then that they appeared. Pointing Hubble into a dark void of space, they discovered *hundreds of billions* of never-before-seen *galaxies*! Not hundreds of billions of never-before-seen stars, but galaxies! Inside a typical galaxy, like the Milky Way, is an estimated one hundred billion stars.

The conclusion of this particular discovery was that there are more stars in the universe than all the grains of sand on the earth's beaches. The discovery

---

3 Westerlund 2, Oct. 14, 2016, Colour Print, 1041x780 px, X-ray: NASA/CXC/SAO/Sejong Univ./ Hur et al; Optical: NASA/STScI, accessed February 14, 2020, https://www.nasa.gov/mission_pages/ chandra/westerlund-2.html

4 Ethan Siegel, "This Is How We Know There Are Two Trillion Galaxies In The Universe," Forbes online, October 18, 2018, https://www.forbes.com/sites/startswithabang/2018/10/18/this-is-how-we-know-there-are-two-trillion-galaxies-in-the-universe/#7557e46e5a67

led astronomists to update their estimate of galaxies in the universe from one hundred seventy billion to two trillion. Not two trillion stars, but two trillion galaxies, each with billions of stars and numerous moons, planets, and heavenly bodies inside of them.

What an unfathomably incredible, awesome creation! But this is far from the most extravagant revelation. In the narrative of Scripture, you can almost breeze over the immensity of Ruach Elohim's creativity, because the writers of Genesis, Job, the psalmists, and later other biblical writers state these parts of the creation in such a matter of fact way: "It was all made by the breath of His mouth" (Ps. 33:6). The wonder of our universe, the planets, heavens, and stars will continue to baffle humanity year after year as we unpack more of their mystery. Yet in all its extravagance, the universe is not the part of creation to be most marveled at. For there was a far more stunning creation which God had not yet revealed.

Indeed, the universe was crowned with glory and filled with wonder by the Father, Son, and Holy Spirit. But then They created their masterpiece.

SCRIPTURE REFERENCES:

"All things were made by him; and without him was not any thing made that was made." (John 1:3 KJV)

"For ever since the world was created, people have seen the earth and sky. Through everything God made, they can clearly see his invisible qualities—his eternal power and divine nature. So they have no excuse for not knowing God." (Rom. 1:20 NLT)

"In His hand are the deep places of the earth;
The heights of the hills are His also.
The sea is His, for He made it;
And His hands formed the dry land." (Ps. 95:4–5 NKJV)

"By faith we understand that the universe was formed at God's command, so that what is seen was not made out of what was visible." (Heb. 11:3 NIV)

CHAPTER 2

THE FIRST BREATH

"For we are God's masterpiece. He has created us anew in Christ Jesus, so we can do the good things he planned for us long ago."

— Ephesians 2:10 NLT

Breathe in the aroma of a million fresh flowers. They have just sprung up in response to the Word of God with their perfectly shaped petals and glossy stems. Inside each one are the seeds of every flower that will ever bloom on the earth.

He is there in the midst of it all. The Beginning and the End. The Alpha and the Omega. The tree branches and tall grass sway gently as Ruach Elohim approaches the Garden of Eden, sending a gentle wave of energy through the oasis, causing birds' wings to perk up. Suddenly, the attention of every living thing is transfixed. For as Ruach Elohim hovers and then touches down on the earth, the Spirit of God transforms into the Ancient of Days, the Almighty, taking the form of Yahweh in the likeness of a man. But not man as we imagine him. This is the form of a man, yes, but overtaking Him is glory so bright that none of the animals can even fully see His face. He has robes concealing His radiant glory, but His face shines brighter than the sun on a cloudless day. He touches down beside the pure, crystalline water that exits Eden in four directions, making the undeniable shape of a cross. Yahweh walks to the centre of Eden, stopping in the shade of the tree of life. The water itself seems to slow down, the particles leaning in as Yahweh's hand reaches down, touching the clay for the first time.

The dirt near the river makes for the best material, pliable yet firm as it soaks up some of the moisture from the river.

He forms an image with heaps of soil and fiber beneath His bent knee, His mouth turned upward in a smile as if He carries a great secret. The earth gives way beneath His hands, His fingernails becoming sullied in the softness of the virgin soil. His hands are calloused yet somehow unworn. They have witnessed ages pass by, yet they are still soft and warm, like the tender palm of a young father grasping the hand of his son.

For the first moment in history, Yahweh can be seen by the rest of creation in a position of vulnerability, getting His hands dirty in the mud, slime, and dust of the earth. This is Father God, the sculptor.

As He gently digs and forms the dirt, an image begins to form on the ground. Remarkably, it takes on His character, His shape . . . though it is only dust.

In the beginning of Genesis, after Ruach Elohim has painted the canvas of the earth, the galaxies, and the universe, we meet two of the most important characters in human history: Adam and Eve. The story of Adam and Eve is fascinating on so many different levels. As a filmmaker interested in digging up the roots of creativity, I've been diving into Scripture for years to find all the references I can about God the Creator.

I'm fascinated by the depiction of Ruach Elohim, the Creator of the universe, as an artist. In most of the creation story of Genesis 1, God is speaking everything into existence, telling planets and matter to do incredible things, forming the stars, aligning the sun and the moon, and commanding light to be separated from darkness. Whatever God declares, happens. But when it comes time for the creation of man and woman, Ruach Elohim takes the form of Yahweh. Ruach Elohim travels through Earth's atmosphere from a hovering vantage point overlooking the expanse of creation, arriving in the intimacy of a garden.

It's incredibly significant that in Genesis 1 the author uses the name Ruach Elohim to describe the Spirit of God, but in Genesis 2 the author matches the intimacy of the garden setting with an intimately new name for God. The Lord

God described in Genesis 2 from English translations comes from the Hebrew name Yahweh (YHWH).

While Genesis 1 repeatedly refers to God as Ruach Elohim, Genesis 2:7 (NIV) starts by saying, "Then the Lord God [YHWH or Yahweh] formed a man . . ."

Before we talk more about God's mysterious new name suddenly being used for the first time, what interests me is the word for "formed," which comes from the Hebrew word *yaw-tsar*. The word literally means "through the squeezing into shape, to mould into a form; especially as a potter; figuratively, to determine, fashion, form, frame, as a potter, to purpose."[5]

One other critical note of context for this story is found in the genealogy from Luke 3:37–38 (NIV, emphasis added), where it says, "the son of Methuselah, the son of Enoch, the son of Jared, the son of Mahalaleel, the son of Cainan, the son of Enos, the son of Seth, *the son of Adam, the son of God.*"

Yahweh was Adam's actual Father, as we see in the genealogy from Luke. The author describes God squeezing Adam into shape from the dust of the earth as a potter or a sculptor works with clay, sculpting him from the clay of the ground. He gives him the name Adam, which sounds like the Hebrew word *adamah*, meaning "dirt." Within His garden studio, Yahweh is found at the height of creative expression, sculpting His masterpiece. For that is what Adam was. A marvel, a sign, and a wonder.

It's hard to fully imagine just how perfectly beautiful Adam and Eve would have been. They were sculpted by the hands of Yahweh Himself! There is not one flaw in the Almighty, so the form and beauty of Adam and Eve would have been awe-inspiring. Their image reflected the glory of a Creator who has the power to breathe stars and galaxies out of His mouth.

However, while there was dimension and impeccable beauty in the sculpted form of the first Adam's body, and even though Yahweh's hands had shaped him, Adam still wasn't *alive.*

Until God the Father breathed on him. The breath of Yahweh gave Adam his first breath. This was the First Breath that shaped humanity.

---

5 Manni Edwards, The Making of a Vessel for Honour (Bloomington, IN: Xlibris, 2018).

"Then the Lord God formed a man from the dust of the
ground and *breathed into his nostrils the breath of life,* and the
man became a living being." (Gen. 2:7 NIV, emphasis added)

The breath of life animated man who was dust into a living being, and this
was the moment when man truly began to bear the image of God: the moment
the breath of Yahweh brought him to life. Made in God's image meant being
alive, because Adam now breathed the same *ruach, breath, spirit* that God
Himself breathes. God is Spirit, as we see in John 4:24 (NKJV): "God is Spirit,
and those who worship Him must worship in spirit and truth."

The verse can also be translated into English as, "God is Breath." And so, the
Spirit of God, His breath, His life force, is imparted to Adam, and Adam becomes
a living being. The first breath of Adam is the inhale of the very presence of
Almighty God. Hundreds of millions of invisible molecules from Yahweh enter
Adam's being. What did that feel like?

The First Breath of God that shaped humanity was literally mankind's first
breath. For Yahweh, it was the first moment in all creation where the Creator was
the One waiting in anticipation of what would happen next.

I've heard it said on many occasions that true creativity comes with a
massive risk.

Cre·a·tiv·i·ty (noun)

1.   The use of the imagination or original ideas, especially in the
production of an artistic work.[6]

The Word of God Himself awaits His creation's first word.

Yahweh pauses, taking one last look at His sculpted masterpiece. He inhales
and then blasts the very first man's face with divine inspiration. His breath comes
like a mighty wind into the soul of Adam. Yet it is no ordinary breath. This breath
is from inside God Himself, an impartation of His living self, into mankind. The
breath or spirit of Yahweh imparted to Adam is what makes him alive.

---

6 Lexico, s.v. "creativity," accessed May 8, 2020, https://www.lexico.com/en/definition/creativity

Quite literally, an impartation of Ruach Elohim is in the breath of Yahweh. The miracle Yahweh imparts to Adam is *neshawmaw* in Hebrew.

Can you hear it?
NESHAWMAW . . .
"A puff of wind, a vital breath, divine inspiration."
"A blast, inspiration, soul, spirit."

From the breath of the living God, man takes in his first breath and becomes a living soul. In this moment we see how the breath and spirit are wholly connected. With his first inhaled breath, the spirit of man comes alive.

> "And the LORD God formed man of the dust of the ground,
> and breathed into his nostrils the breath of life [*neshawmaw*];
> and man became a living soul." (Gen. 2:7 KJV)

What a moment. The moment the breath of every living human being became automatic. The First Breath from Yahweh into Adam caused his chest to rise and fall for the first time, and by extension it automated the rise and fall of the lungs of every living soul since Adam. Every breath taken by humanity became automated in that moment until each person's final breath, which exhales their spirit out of their body. Even if a person tries to hold their breath and says, "I will not breathe again," that person will automatically breathe again within a few short seconds.

Try it right now. You will most likely need another breath in thirty seconds or less. Even if a person is under water and knows that their next breath will bring water into their lungs and they will drown, still a person's breathing continues.

The Hebrew word *neshawmaw* is recorded twenty-four times in the Old Testament, beginning with the creation of Adam in Genesis 2:7. In English the translation is "breath" or "breath of life." Once again, the Hebrew text unveils much more meaning than the English translation. In Hebrew, the power of story and words have added layers of verbiage describing many of our English words as actions. The vital breath of the LORD God is described as His powerful life force being stirred up and blown not only into Adam's nostrils, but breathed upon Adam's face and breathed upon his very being. It's more like a fully charged defibrillator to the life force of man than just a breath. It's a stirred up, creative Yahweh bringing Adam's vital signs to life. And this First Breath of the Lord into the face and nostrils and lungs of Adam is a holy breath, imparted by the Holy God.

The breath of life comes from Yahweh the Giver of Life, Ruach Elohim, Giver of Spirits. Remember that the Spirit of God from Genesis 1, Ruach Elohim, takes the form of Yahweh in the Garden. So, Genesis 2:7 more accurately says in English, "And Yahweh breathed into his nostrils the breath of life and the man became a living being." I find this passage to be an incredible revelation. When Father God breathes on Adam, he is actually blowing hundreds of billions of breaths, because every breath EVER is connected to the power of a single YAH . . . WEH.

The English name of Yahweh, which is believed to be the most accurate pronunciation of God's name, comes from the four characters in Hebrew that translate in English to YHWH. When we add the vowels to this essentially unpronounceable name, we get Yahweh. But from the Hebrew we find that His name may only be properly understood using the sound of breath!

Yod: the Hebrew letter translated to *Y* in English starts with a dramatic pause, symbolizing purpose and intention.

He (pronounced *hey*): the Hebrew letter translated to *H* in English; this is the inhaled breath of Yahweh.

Waw: the Hebrew translated to *W* in English; this is where the breath sits within the lungs for a moment as the oxygen begins to move into the heart and distributes throughout the body.

He: a second He, which is the exhaled breath blown upon the face of Adam.

To simplify the process, say it out loud in English. *YAHWEH.* First an inhale: YAH (pronounced *yaah*). Next an exhale: WEH (pronounced *way*).

Do you see it? The name of God is in the actual breath itself! Ruach Elohim takes the form of Yahweh when He breathes on Adam in the Garden of Eden. The first gift and impartation from the Living God to make a living man is His NAME. There is power in His name to bring the lifeless to life.

From the moment I discovered this until now, whenever I think of the magnitude of God imparting His name to humanity, bringing mankind to life, I am in awe. His name is the Word and the Word of God literally imparts life to our spirits.

This is a gift so regularly given and received that many of us fail to recognize its presence altogether. Every breath from the creation of Adam until this moment has been a form of uttering the name of Yahweh, His holy name. Just pause to consider the enormity of this: Every breath, ever, is an utterance of your Creator's name.

Breath is sometimes described as more of a whisper than a word, but it can be characterized as a form of speech. In a story about the Prophet Elijah in 1 Kings, a still, small voice comes to Elijah and is described as a whisper, a breath.

> "After the earthquake there was a fire, but the LORD
> [YAHWEH] was not in the fire. And after the fire there was a
> voice, a soft whisper." (1 Kings 19:12 HCSB)

Think of it as the quiet utterance of His own name. Yahweh was in the voice, the whisper, the breath.

And so it was with Adam. The first whisper or breath of man is an utterance of the name of his Creator. Like the worship song by Bryan and Katie Torwalt from Jesus Culture, "I breathe You in God, because You are thick all around me." What an incredible gift. The neshawmaw breath from the Spirit of Yahweh is what makes humanity image-bearers of Yahweh. The gift of His life-giving name then enters mankind's DNA. The gift is then passed down by all the billions of people ever created.

When Eve, which means "mother of all the living," bore her first son in Genesis 4:1 (NET), she said, "I have created a man just as the LORD [Yahweh] did!" Adam and Eve, image-bearers of Yahweh, were given the ability to create offspring who also breathed the neshawmaw breath of life. This is a clear example of mankind bearing God's image and passing that image along to their offspring.

So, in what "spirit" or attitude do we choose to breathe His name? Do we bless and honour His holy name as we breathe our way through life, or do we curse and dishonour it?

To the Hebrews, the name of God was so holy that it could not even be spoken aloud out of reverence for the name of the One who gave them breath. To speak His name in vain was to blaspheme His name. And if blasphemed, according to Jewish Law in the Torah, the blasphemer was under penalty of death.

The name that gives life, if misrepresented, would lead to your death.

Hundreds of years after Adam, Moses encounters the living God, God's Spirit in the bush on Mount Sinai that is burning but not consumed. This is more than just an incredible physical encounter and experience between God and man. This is also the moment when God tells Moses His name.

> "And God answered unto Moses, I AM THAT I AM. And
> He said, Thus shalt thou say unto the sons of Israel: I AM
> [YHWH] has sent me unto you." (Exod. 3:14 JUB)

The name God tells Moses to use when people ask for His name is I AM, and this deserves repeating: In the letter form it becomes the word we pronounce by adding two vowels in English—YAHWEH. The Y-H-W-H letter form of His name is referred to as the tetragrammaton (from the Greek), meaning "consisting of four letters." And where observant Jews following Talmudic Jewish tradition find these letters in the Hebrew Bible and the Torah, they will not pronounce these four characters out loud. They do not even read out loud the proposed transcriptions in the forms of Yahweh or Yehovah, but out of reverence for the Holy name of God, they substitute the tetragrammaton with *Adonai*, meaning "My Lord," *Hashem*, meaning "The Name," or *hakadosh baruch hu*, meaning "The Holy One, Blessed Be He."

But from the time Moses first learned to speak Yahweh's name out loud until present day, a massive truth has been missed by millions of people: We were born to be connected to Yahweh as surely as we breathe the sound of His name. The One who breathed life over Adam was Father God, the eternal I AM, the Breath of Life, the Creator of all who is *in all*. His name is Yahweh!

If you wanted to get into the physiology, you could say that this breath informs every decision of your brain, every impulse of your neurons, every action of your body. Because without your next breath, your next "Yah . . . weh" (for that is the sound you whisper when you breathe), you would not have any oxygen in your blood—the activity needed to make your next movement or decision.

Ephesians 4:4–6 (NIV, emphasis added) says, "There is one body and one Spirit, just as you were called to one hope when you were called; one Lord, one faith, one baptism; *one God and Father of all, who is over all and through all and in all.*"

For the first time I realized that He is literally in all. Yahweh is the Alpha and Omega, the First and the Last. The first breath of every human being is inhaled as a whisper of the name of Yahweh. The last breath of every human being is exhaled as a final utterance of the name of Yahweh, returning our spirit, our breath, back to Yahweh. He's the Alpha and the Omega. He gets the first and last word.

I realized that so many of my fellow believers have missed a great deal about Yahweh's character and power. One reason is simply that most people, particularly in North America and Europe, have only ever read about or referred to the name of God as LORD. Sadly, the name of our Creator has been lost to so many. Realizing that God, who is Spirit, breathed upon humanity His very essence—imparting Himself and His name, Yahweh, into humanity—seems tremendously important to me when considering that the Bible says, "So God created man in His own image; in the image of God He created him; male and female He created them" (Genesis 1:27 NKJV). The breath of His Spirit (and name) is where our resemblance to Yahweh comes from. His Spirit and breath are the very thing keeping us alive, bearing His likeness.

It's not only a heartwarming idea I am sharing with you, but the First Breath of Yahweh is literally the breath that to this day keeps humanity alive. After that, humanity did not somehow begin to breathe independently of the neshawmaw, upholding life on their own power as so many believe.

The Book of Job speaks to a deeper understanding that people had about creation and the Garden of Eden in time past. They knew that Yahweh's breath of life upheld the flesh and kept humanity alive. They also understood that when this breath was removed from the flesh, what remained was only a corpse that returned to dust.

Job said in Job 34:14–15 (NASB), "If He should determine to do so, if He should gather to Himself His spirit and His breath [*neshawmaw*], all flesh would perish together, and man would return to dust."

Yahweh told this to Adam and Eve in Genesis 3:19 (ESV): "By the sweat of your face you shall eat bread, till you return to the ground, for out of it you were taken; for you are dust, and to dust you shall return."

Solomon too, the wisest man who ever lived, spoke about the breath of life and man's return to dust: "Before the dust returns to the ground from which it came, and the spirit returns to God who gave it" (Eccles. 12:7 BSB).

In the absence of the repetitive utterance of Yahweh's name, which is on our breath and gives life to our spirits, we are literally only dust.

The idea of silently speaking Yahweh's name when we breathe also got me thinking about the third commandment that Yahweh wrote with His own hand on the tablets of stone given to Moses.

> "You shall not take the name of the Lord your God in vain,
> for the Lord will not hold him guiltless who takes His name in
> vain." (Exod. 20:7 NKJV)

The original text says, "You shall not take in vain the name of your God *YHWH* [*Yahweh*]. For *YHWH* [*Yahweh*] will not hold him guiltless that takes his name in vain."

It's not hard for me to imagine that this commandment means more than any child has ever been taught in Sunday school. The idea that swearing with God's name is the fullness of this command falls way short of Yahweh's glory. I cringe when people effortlessly curse and use His holy name in vain, and sometimes I even turn off a movie when I hear His name used so recklessly, but there is much more to this commandment. Contrary to the way it's presented by many as a "forgettable and easy commandment to keep," it may in fact be the most difficult of all the Ten Commandments to live by.

Jesus repeatedly taught that the words and actions of mankind were only indicators of the true self, which is the spirit or heart of a person.

If you're familiar with the Sermon on the Mount from the Book of Matthew, it's clear that the standards of God are out of reach for us, humanly speaking. Jesus actually lays out a standard of living that is unattainable except for in relationship with Him and the working of The Holy Spirit in our lives, which at the time of His teaching had not yet been given. After Jesus preached these kinds of sermons, He *lost* followers; He didn't gain them.

In the Sermon on the Mount, Jesus equates anger toward a brother or sister to murder. He also equates lust in a person's heart to adultery. He lays out a case that convicts every human being (past, present, future) as guilty of sin. He proves that we need a savior and sets the stage for our desperately needed redemption.

So when I consider the commandment about the name of Yahweh, I tremble, because *we quietly speak His name with our every breath.* And the way in which we breathe His name is either an act of worship, in spirit and truth, or by misusing of His name under your breath, an act of taking His name in vain.

Consider Paul the apostle. Thirteen of the twenty-seven books in the New Testament are attributed to Paul. His conversion experience on the Road to Damascus was incredible, and his life in ministry was extraordinary. Paul, the great man of God! Paul, the healer and apostle!

But for a long time before he preached the Gospel of Jesus, Paul (whose name was Saul at the time) was an enemy of Yahweh living under the curse of sin. It says in Acts 9:1–2 (NIV, emphasis added), "Meanwhile, Saul was still *breathing out* murderous threats against the Lord's disciples. He went to the high priest and asked him for letters to the synagogues in Damascus, so that if he found any there who belonged to the Way, whether men or women, he might take them as prisoners to Jerusalem."

Interesting language: "Breathing out murderous threats." The author's message is that Saul was profanely speaking Yahweh's name with every breath, because Saul's very spirit was corrupted by sin and therefore his actual breath was murder and a self-condemning act of blasphemy. The great man of God was taking the name of his Creator in vain.

I like how the New Living Translation puts it as well: "Meanwhile, Saul was uttering threats *with every breath* and was eager to kill the Lord's followers" (emphasis added).

Do you know that you are capable of breathing out murder and threats as surely as you breathe? We have power to breathe good as well as evil.

The aspects of Paul the apostle's life that many emphasize are undoubtedly his life and ministry and the many miracles that took place in the decades following his unusual conversion. I typically think about Paul as a performer of miracles, a man on fire for God. My personal favourite is that Yahweh used Paul's sweaty handkerchiefs and dirty towels to heal people (Acts 19:11–12). But the same man who wrote half of the books of the New Testament was breathing murder for a long time before he did any breathing for Christ. This should amaze and also inspire us, reminding us that every soul on earth can choose to follow either the kingdom of this world or the Kingdom of Yahweh.

In what spirit are you breathing His name? I believe the third commandment is saying that you are guilty of blaspheming the Almighty name of Yahweh even if you *breathe* in vain. Furthermore, to misuse His name, as many do through falsely representing Him or utilizing His name for personal benefit, is taking His name in vain. To take His holy name in vain is to bring condemnation on yourself. Oh, how we need a Savior!

There is no name that is holy besides the Lord God's (Yahweh's), Jesus', and The Holy Spirit's. While Yahweh's name is clearly emphasized as holy in the Ten Commandments, remember that the Father, Son, and Holy Spirit are ONE. How we breathe Yahweh's name reveals our heart about Jesus and The Holy Spirit as well.

The name of Yahweh was so revered in the time that Jesus walked the earth, that on several occasions He was accused of blasphemy by those who did not believe Jesus was the Son of Yahweh. One of my favorite Scriptures of all features the claim of Jesus that He is in fact one with Yahweh and that He existed from the beginning with Yahweh.

Jesus said to them, "Most assuredly, I say to you, before Abraham was, I AM." (John 8:58 NKJV)

Jesus was most likely speaking Hebrew or Aramaic when He spoke these unforgettable words, meaning the name of YAH (short form of Yahweh) was on His lips. "Saying this, they picked up stones to stone Him" (v. 59). The claim was unthinkable to His listeners. The context was that Jesus pre-existed Abraham, their most adored forefather. A simple-looking man standing before them in his early thirties was claiming to be equal and pre-existent with Yahweh, and He was using language similar to when Yahweh told Moses His name at the burning bush. Jesus was declaring, with the sound of His breath, that He was I AM. To be there when He spoke these words! Yet the world did not recognize Him.

John's Gospel is largely dedicated to proving that Jesus is the promised Messiah. And here, Jesus makes an outstanding claim that aligns with the first words of John's Gospel: "In the beginning was the Word, and the Word was with God, and the Word was God. He was with God in the beginning" (John 1:1–2 NIV).

There is a fascinating grace and wisdom from Yahweh in the revelation of His name being spoken through our breath. First of all, it transcends language. The names of God are translated and transliterated in all languages; however, the name of Yahweh, our Breath of Life, is not a word, but rather an expression that humanity shares in exactly the same way. With every breath, the name of Yahweh is available to all who are made in His image. Even after the time of Babel, when the earth was divided into people groups that spoke different languages, Yahweh's name remains humanity's life force and daily breath. Today there are more than 6,500 spoken languages, but only one Breath of Life.

One Rabbi further explained that if you try to say Yahweh's name with speech, you actually are unable to do it accurately. The letters transliterated to YHWH are one part vowel and one part consonant. **When said without adding vowels, a person must simply breathe.**

NOTE TO READER:

Throughout this book, God the Father will primarily be referred to as Yahweh or YHWH, particularly when quoting the original Scriptures, which used His proper name as YHWH. In most English translations today, *Yahweh* has been replaced with *Lord* or *Lord God*, but the original text typically used Yahweh (in the letter form from Hebrew, which would translate to YHWH or YHVH; to say it in English, vowels needed to be added, making the name appear as Yahweh, Yahovah, or Yehovah. Jehovah with a *J* was only added to some translations later after the letter *J* came into the lexicon in the 1500s.

Every time you read His name as Yahweh in the Scriptures quoted throughout this book, I encourage you to consider the significance of His name as Yahweh, your Giver of breath.

CHAPTER 3

CORRUPTING THE BREATH

Dust began to rise like a storm cloud around Jerusalem. The sound of ten thousand instruments rose higher still. Harps, lyres, and flutes gave way to drums and crashing cymbals. A general seasoned by Israel's wars commanded the front line to play a melody that rose above the dust, straight to Heaven. A procession of hundreds was flanked by hundreds of thousands of onlookers. It seemed the entire nation had come to celebrate. The road to Jerusalem was lined with palm branches, and young girls placed roses and lilies on the path before King David's feet. Stirred by the beautiful fragrance of rose petals and the heavenly orchestrations of the chief musician, David removed his kingly robe. Underneath, he wore merely a linen garment that matched the sleeveless garments of the priests. Freed from the weight of his robes, he began to dance. While young maidens watched in wonder, the mighty men of King David's army watched him too, overwhelmed by the display. David was recklessly abandoned in worship. There was a notable shift in the atmosphere; while some scorned the act as undignified, others joined in, worshiping and dancing along with their king.

Somehow the music and the cries of joy from the people made the gold-plated Ark of the Covenant light upon the Levites' shoulders. It was as if the hundreds of pounds of gold were merely hovering. For a moment, perhaps the burden they carried was carrying them, for inside they sensed the presence of the very Mystery that brought Adam to life in the Garden of Eden. Shouts of joy vibrated the foundations of the city as young and old declared, "Hallelujah! The Ark of our God, Yahweh has returned. The Ark that our Creator chose to dwell in. God is with us!"

David understood the deep desire of Yahweh in the Garden of Eden: That our breath of life, neshawmaw, our very spirit, was created to fellowship *constantly* with Yahweh. We breathe constantly thanks to Yahweh, and we were created to praise constantly through fellowship with the Spirit of God (Ruach Elohim). Psalm 150 is about praising Yahweh with our life—our words and our daily walk being the greatest asset we can bring to Him in worship.

Consider in a new way the final pen stroke or verse from the Book of Psalms. In Psalm 150:6 (ISV), the psalmist King David concludes, "Let everyone who breathes praise the LORD. Hallelujah!"

Hallelujah is a compound word from the Hebrew of *hallelu* and *Yah*, meaning "Praise Yahweh!" In its originally described form, *hallelujah* can be understood to mean, "Let us praise Yah, the breath of life!"

The name for LORD in Hebrew written by David in this verse was the shortened form of Yahweh, "YAH." Each inhale of Yah's name is meant to make us exhale with our spirit saying, "Hallelujah." Whether a person is aware of it or not, this is a natural process made possible with every breath. The psalmist is describing that Yahweh gives us purpose for every breath that we breathe, and that purpose is praise. What David essentially concludes is that every "Yah" that we breathe makes us say, "Hallelujah!" There is literally rhyme and reason to the statement. The inhale of Yah's name (which we whisper as we breathe) makes us shout or exhale praise using YAHWEH'S NAME!

Furthermore, Strong's concordance describes the word *praise* that David uses in the Hebrew to mean, "making one's boast, making a fool of, to act madly or like a madman."[7] This is an offensive level of praise that David himself showcased when he brought the Ark of the LORD (YHWH) into Jerusalem.

> "And David danced before the LORD [YHWH] with all his
> might, wearing a priestly garment. So David and all the people
> of Israel brought up the Ark of the Lord with shouts of joy and
> the blowing of rams' horns." (2 Sam. 6:14–15 NLT)

---

7 NET Bible, s.v. "halal," accessed May 8, 2020, http://classic.net.bible.org/strong.php?id=01984

As the holy name of God comes into our bodies through our breath, our inner spiritual being was created to come alive with worship.

> "But as the Ark of the LORD [YHWH] entered the City of David, Michal, the daughter of Saul, looked down from her window. When she saw King David leaping and dancing before the LORD [YHWH], she was filled with contempt for him." (2 Sam. 6:16 NLT)

As we see from the response of Michal toward King David, not everyone is converting their breath into praise. We need to go back to Genesis to find the reason for Michal's reaction to her husband. For a time on earth there was perfect order in creation, until Adam and Eve brought sin into their DNA and passed that down to every human being after them. Since then, there has been a catch. Each person is now faced with a decision, of their own free will: which atmosphere their spirit breathes and resides in.

Without recognizing the fall of Adam and Eve in the Garden of Eden, we return to the same question over and over again: If the breath of Yahweh is in all of humanity, why is there so much wrong with the world? This question has been renewed in our generation, as so many have walked away from relationship with Yahweh.

Particularly in North American and European cultures, another question asked frequently by people is, "How can God be real, or how can God be good if so much bad or evil is allowed to happen?" The evil referred to in this context is almost always a reference to external forces or spirits that attack people and their loved ones or attack the things a person loves or values in life. The evil at work in the world is called sin, and all forms of evil result from the fruit of sin and darkness.

According to the historical definition, *sin* is "a word, deed, or desire in opposition to the eternal law of God (Yahweh)." It was not long after Yahweh breathed life into His beautiful sculpture of Adam, that humanity turned from God, according to Genesis 6:5–6 (WEB, emphasis added): "Yahweh saw that the wickedness of man was great in the earth, and that every imagination of the thoughts of his heart was only evil continually. *Yahweh was sorry that he had made man on the earth, and it grieved him in his heart."*

A few minutes watching the evening news, a walk through certain parts of your city, or a few moments of introspection will bring to your mind and heart the evidence of sin. Abuse, sexual immorality, lying, stealing, disease, human trafficking, envy, jealousy. Sin takes many different forms. Even without going to extremes, we feel and see the results of sin in some of our relationships, in offences we carry, and in our encounters with personal shame or fear. But it has become more and more rare for people to admit where they have made agreements with evil in their own lives. Can we admit the areas of our lives where we have blasphemed or dishonoured or taken in vain the name of Yahweh?

We were made in Yahweh's image. We have breath (a spirit) and we have a heart (I'm referring to the spiritual heart) because Yahweh does. The heart of our Creator was grieved by the consistent and total corruption that had flooded the hearts of man, which were only evil continually. By using the word "continually," the text reminds us that they were sinning with every breath.

There had to be a new plan put into place. There had to be a restoration of the breath of man, and the heart of man would need to be transplanted. The darkness upon the earth would need to be literally washed away, and the earth would need to be cleansed.

> "For from within the hearts of men come evil thoughts, sexual immorality, theft, murder, adultery." (Mark 7:21 BSB)

I've been seeing the evidence of sin in some of its ugliest manifestations while producing recent films about human trafficking and sexual slavery. My brothers and I released a film in 2016 called *She Has A Name*, inspired by true events in Southeast Asia. It tells the story of two fifteen-year-old girls trafficked in a seafood container across international borders. Sadly, it is just one story of millions like it. The corruption of the spirit of man because of sin is darker than I wanted to imagine. The pain and suffering that sin creates is devastating. Darkness can turn the brilliant God-given imaginations of man into pure, unfathomable evil.

One of the moments that prompted me to write this book happened on October 6, 2019. I was woken suddenly because a large wooden barn door in between our bedroom and bathroom was suddenly, inexplicably open. The door is not only large but also heavy, and when left opened, a lot of natural light floods into our bedroom, so the door is consistently kept closed. My wife and I get up to close it if left open, because we choose to sleep in extreme darkness (evidenced by the many creative ways in which we block every shaft of light from entering our room at night and put tape or clothing over those annoying red lights on electronics). But suddenly I was awake, and that large sliding barn door was wide open. For some reason the first thing I thought of was the door on the Ark in the story of Noah and the flood. Then I heard what I can best describe as an audible voice, like a whisper, say simply, "Seven, twenty-two." I looked over at the open door and said, "What do You mean by seven, twenty-two?" The response I heard whispered back was, "Genesis 7:22." I looked at my clock and the time was exactly 7:20. So I decided to open my Bible on the bedside table and read Genesis 7 from verses 20–22, the story of Noah and the flood. It is perhaps the most powerful biblical story depicting the end result of mankind turning from Yahweh, and this time I read it like I had never read it before:

> "The waters rose and covered the mountains to a depth of more than fifteen cubits. Every living thing that moved on land perished—birds, livestock, wild animals, all the creatures that swarm over the earth, and all mankind. Everything on dry land that had the breath of life [neshawmaw] in its nostrils died" (NIV).

I was blown away (pardon the pun). I had just been trying to dig into Scriptures about breath. And there it was again—the *neshawmaw*. The breath Adam inhaled in the Garden of Eden was here in the story of Noah and the flood.

And so, in Genesis 7:22 Yahweh takes back the breath of life from all humanity—except he doesn't take His breath, the ability to declare His name, back from Noah and his family, who were found righteous in their generation.

They found favour, grace, and salvation from Yahweh because they were breathing differently than everyone else.

Genesis 6:9 (NIV) says, "This is the account of Noah and his family. Noah was a righteous man, blameless among the people of his time, and he walked faithfully with God."

But everyone else who had the breath of the spirit of life, died.

From a simplified point of view, the flood was about cleansing and purifying the breath of life, to restore it closer to the form in which Yahweh gave it in Eden. But on top of that, there were other influences, other spirits at work on the earth in those days. Part of the story of the flood was that Satan and his angels (demons) were on the earth corrupting the image of God that was made by Yahweh.

There was a ground-level spiritual attack in full swing during the time of Noah's flood. Satan had invaded the earth with rebellious angels, and they were making every effort to corrupt the seed of the woman, Eve, so that the seed of the prophetically significant "second Eve," Mary, would be corrupted. From the time of Adam and Eve's sin in the Garden of Eden, Yahweh had clearly outlined His plan of salvation: "He shall bruise your head, and you shall bruise His heel" (Gen. 3:15 NKJV).

Genesis 6:3–5 (BSB) says, "So the LORD [YAHWEH] said, 'My Spirit will not contend with man forever, for he is mortal; his days shall be 120 years.' The Nephilim were on the earth in those days, and afterward as well, when the sons of God had relations with the daughters of men. And they bore them children who became the mighty men of old, men of renown. Then the LORD [YAHWEH] saw that the wickedness of man was great upon the earth, and that every inclination of the thoughts of his heart was altogether evil all the time . . ."

Satan understands the power and significance of the neshawmaw breath of life. His rage and hate for humanity is wrapped up first in his hate for Yahweh because he was unable to rise to the level of glory that Yahweh is worthy of and will always have:

"How you have fallen from heaven, O star of the morning, son of the dawn! You have been cut down to the earth, you who have weakened the nations! But you said in your heart, 'I will ascend to heaven; I will raise my throne above the stars of God, And I will sit on the mount of assembly in the recesses of the north. I will ascend above the heights of the clouds; I will make myself like the Most High.'" (Isa. 14:12–15 NASB)

Satan therefore hates humanity because man was made in the image of Yahweh. Man received Yahweh's breath. Angels and supernatural beings, despite their power or authority in heavenly realms, are spirits that have a specific purpose assigned to them.

Regarding Yahweh's angels, Paul writes in Hebrews 1:13–14 (BSB), "Yet to which of the angels did God ever say: 'Sit at My right hand until I make Your enemies a footstool for Your feet'? Are not the angels ministering spirits sent to serve those who will inherit salvation?"

Regarding Satan and his angels, it says in Luke 10:17–20 (NIV): "The seventy-two returned with joy and said, 'Lord, even the demons submit to us in your name.' He replied, 'I saw Satan fall like lightning from heaven. I have given you authority to trample on snakes and scorpions and to overcome all the power of the enemy; nothing will harm you. However, do not rejoice that the spirits submit to you, but rejoice that your names are written in heaven.'"

I experienced a version of this Scripture in a vision I had one night when putting our daughter Rosie to bed. At the time, Rosie was about a year old, and we were visiting my parents for a holiday. I was in my old bedroom in my parents' basement, rocking my baby to sleep. That very room was my bedroom for nineteen years, so I spent an immense amount of my life there. It was one of the places I built history and relationship with Yahweh. Every night I would pray as I went to sleep, and one of my prayers, which I still pray to this day as I go to sleep, was "Thank you, Jesus, for dreams about You, about Heaven, and about Your angels." I was praying something similar over my daughter Rosie as I rocked her to sleep that night, and I was looking at her beautiful face when it happened. In a split second, literally in the blink of an eye, I had an encounter with Heaven. What I saw in that split second somehow lasted for minutes in Heaven. I was suddenly in an immensely large hall, and although it doesn't do it justice, I will try to provide a visualization. It was like a scene from *The Fellowship of the Ring*, where the fellowship finds themselves in the halls of Moria underground. Gandalf raises his staff, glowing with magical light, and the camera sweeps through the immense digital landscape of Tolkien's imagined world. Peter Jackson, one of my favorite filmmakers, does well to give us epic moments like this, where we the audience feel the awe and wonder of beauty and imagine the possibilities that our own creativity and stewardship could bring in such a majestically created world. This is before the goblins and evil spirits of Middle-earth descend on the fellowship and Gandalf, at the cost of his own life, must sacrifice all to bring down the ancient evil of the Balrog. I'm sure that more than a few of my fellow *Lord of the Rings* fans can imagine the scene.

Similarly, in this vision I was in an immensely large gathering place. The place was so expansive that it held the spirits of all humanity. In the vision, I could see both a physical likeness of all humanity, and yet all of humanity was in spirit form, like vapors, dancing slowly in their places. They flickered slowly back and forth like candles; the imagery was not dissimilar from how we might imagine a spirit's form based on the depiction of a spirit in films or animation. There were billions upon billions of souls, and they disappeared over the horizon of that immense hall as far as the eye could see.

Suddenly, every soul's attention shifted to an elevated area where there was a throne. The Alpha and Omega, Beginning and End, Yahweh, Jesus Christ, the Living God, was coming forth from His chamber. His glory was indescribable, and all the souls of humanity were looking to Him, completely fixated on His brilliance. There was an energy coming from His being that was light so bright He could scarcely be looked at, and yet we had not even seen His face, only His body, which was covered in robes. He appeared both like a man and as a being over ten feet tall. He was carrying a massive book. He came forward to a large table and, holding the book in front of Him, let it fall from His hands. When it hit the table, a surge of infinite energy went rippling through the place, and all the souls of humanity were flattened to the ground. This too was like a scene from the prologue of *The Fellowship of the Ring*, when the ring of power is cut from Sauron's finger and a sonic boom of energy lays the orcs, elves, and men flat upon the ground. Except this surge laid flat all the billions ever created—past, present, and future. There was a pause while humanity braced from the wave. Suddenly, the glory of Almighty God was so intense that regardless of the effort, not a soul could lift itself up, but all were lying flat, held in place by the glory of the Lord. A whisper began to rise in that place, and the whisper was like a groan from every soul; the same thought, word, and cry was coming from every soul in that chamber. Each one looked, if they could, at the throne of Yahweh and asked the same question, because it was the only question in all of human history that mattered anymore: "Is my name in the Book?"

I had caught a glimpse of the scene from Revelation 20:11–13 (NKJV): "Then I saw a great white throne and Him who sat on it, from whose face the earth and the heaven fled away. And there was found no place for them. And I saw the dead, small and great, standing before God, and books were opened. And another book was opened, which is the Book of Life. And the dead were judged according to their works, by the things which were written in the books. The sea gave up the dead who were in it, and Death and Hades delivered up the dead who were in them. And they were judged, each one according to his works."

At this moment in history, when the great hall of judgment holds the breaths, spirits, souls of all humanity, there will only be one question: Is my name in the Book of Life? Jesus Himself told His disciples to rejoice in nothing else but that their names were written in Heaven. Yes, they could wield better-than-Gandalf authority over principalities and demons, and they could do incredible miracles in Jesus' name, but the pinnacle of their purpose was to have their names written in the Lamb's eternal Book of Life.

There is an enemy that goes about like a roaring lion (but not the Lion of Judah) and like a lamb (but not the Lamb of God, rather a wolf in sheep's clothing). This enemy has come into our atmosphere and polluted the very air that was created by Yahweh for us to breathe.

"And there was war in heaven, Michael and his angels waging
war with the dragon. The dragon and his angels waged war,
and they were not strong enough, and there was no longer
a place found for them in heaven. And the great dragon
was thrown down, the serpent of old who is called the devil
and Satan, who deceives the whole world; he was thrown
down to the earth, and his angels were thrown down with
him." (Rev. 12:7–17 NASB)

Redeemed man, made in Yahweh's image, has the ability to breathe in and
breathe out Yahweh's nature and qualities. This is the ultimate calling of human
beings: to be transformed into the nature of Yahweh and live for Him in a lifestyle
of worship. To worship Him in the Spirit and in truth. To honour His breath with
every part of our physical and spiritual beings. And this only becomes possible
when we repent of our sin (in our DNA since Adam and Eve) and invite The
Holy Spirit in (Ruach ha'Kodesh, whom we will talk about more later).

Satan, on the other hand, blasphemes the name of Yahweh through a series
of counterfeits to the real Spirit and presence of God. When you look at the
stories biblically, as well as the work of spiritual forces of darkness in the world,
you can clearly see the pattern of blasphemy and counterfeit. All the devil can do
is mimic the Creator Yahweh, and in so doing, he corrupts and counterfeits God's
glory, taking Yahweh's name in vain. Satan tries to trap and delude the hearts and
minds of as many spirits inside human beings who will follow him. We will look
at this further throughout the book.

The flood was a global event that communicates two very powerful truths.
First, that Yahweh is the Giver of Breath and He can take back the neshawmaw
breath of life whenever He wills. But the flood also shows us the saving power
of Yahweh and how Yahweh is Ruach Elohim, the Spirit that hovers over the
waters. He invites the righteous into His dwelling place—in the flood story it was
literally an ark, made of wood. This shows us that we can rise above the waters
of judgment and destruction if we put our faith in Him. Thankfully, as His plan
unfolded throughout history, the ark of His presence was made accessible to all
humanity. Every soul who stands before the throne of Yahweh can ensure that

their name is written in the Book of Life through the death and resurrection of Jesus, because the incredible story of Jesus was written before the breath of life was ever given to humanity.

> "And all the people who belong to this world worshiped the beast. *They are the ones whose names were not written in the Book of Life that belongs to the Lamb who was slaughtered before the world was made.*" (Rev. 13:8 NLT, emphasis added)

Last but not least, the flood was meant to save the bloodline through which Jesus, the Savior of the world, would come, conceived by The Holy Spirit. From the time of being cursed in the Garden of Eden by Yahweh, Satan was given a clear enemy and devised his plan of attack: to corrupt the Seed of humanity. Yahweh prophetically declares the fate of humanity and the devil in Genesis 3:15 (NKJV): "And I will put enmity between you and the woman, and between your Seed and her Seed; He shall bruise your head, And you shall bruise His heel."

Eve's Seed, ultimately in the womb of Mary, would conceive Jesus by the power of The Holy Spirit and crush Satan's head. Satan's foreknowledge of the destiny of Eve's Seed would prompt him to commit every assault and blasphemy imaginable through the ages in hopes of corrupting the promised Seed.

That's why the flood is also about protecting the bloodline promised in the Garden of Eden by Yahweh. Yahweh spoke His prophetic declaration that the Seed of the woman will crush the head of the serpent. While the devil is also told that he will cause humanity to limp in the process by bruising the heel of her Seed, it's obvious from the beginning that he has been defeated. But the devil hates losing and has always wanted to undermine his ultimate fate by seeking victory and damaging all he can along the way.

Revelation 12:3–4 (NIV) says, "Then another sign appeared in heaven: an enormous red dragon with seven heads and ten horns and seven crowns on its heads. Its tail swept a third of the stars out of the sky and flung them to the earth. The dragon stood in front of the woman who was about to give birth, so that it might devour her child the moment he was born."

We see the serpent, the dragon Satan, the devil, making it his purpose and goal throughout history to destroy the woman's promised Seed. His and his minions' mission is to crush the hope of salvation and steal the joy and life and breath away from mankind. His mission is to defy the promises and purposes of Yahweh. Is it any surprise, then, that he operates in a different spirit than the Spirit of Yahweh?

The devil had nearly corrupted the Seed at the time of the flood.

Again, Genesis 6:4–5 (BSB) says, "The Nephilim were on the earth in those days, and afterward as well, when the sons of God [angels] had relations with the daughters of men. And they bore them children who became the mighty men of old, men of renown. Then the LORD [Yahweh] saw that the wickedness of man was great upon the earth, and that every inclination of the thoughts of his heart was altogether evil all the time."

Yahweh cleansed the earth and found Noah and his offspring to be the only remaining righteous ones in Noah's generation, and Noah became the carrier of the promised Seed.

The stories of Satan's rebellious and corrupting ways repeat time and again throughout history. We see it at work in the slavery of Israel in Egypt after the death of Joseph. We see it again when the children of Israel are killed in Egypt by Pharaoh during the time of Moses' birth. We see it in the proclamation of King Herod to kill the young children at the time of Jesus' birth. We see it at work again and again through men and women of power, corrupted by the spirit at work in our atmosphere. We see it in how the Jewish people were systematically exterminated during the Holocaust, and even up to the modern-day enmity and hate and outspoken evil will against the Seed of Abraham. Since the coming of Jesus, we see the outrage of the devil continuing against the people of Yahweh and followers of the Way.

But the plan of God continues to outmatch the enemy—the Seed of the woman was not corrupted, and the coming of Jesus was not thwarted. Yahweh wins the ultimate victory, and the power of His Word and His breath will never be overcome.

CHAPTER 4

SATAN AND THE POWER OF THE AIR

I was sitting in the second-to-last row of a full auditorium. Although I was far from the man speaking, it was as if his words were exploding inside my very soul like fireworks. The Spirit of God was absolutely vibrating, and I could feel His creative energy hovering over me. There was truth so deep being fed to me that my inner spiritual man was growing, making me suddenly aware of the connection between my physical being and my spiritual being. Each breath and word seemed to impart a greater sense of God's presence. The preacher was trying his best to share a word from Scripture while Ruach Elohim kept interrupting him. There was not only a rich atmosphere of God's love, but there was warmth and humour and joy in that place. Prophetic words with incredible detail were being shared with complete strangers. Tears were flowing down the faces of young and old, male and female. A lady with extreme pain in her abdomen was healed as she tried approaching the altar. There was an atmosphere of great expectation—the awareness of the Spirit of God in that place was giving me hope and joy while also imparting to others faith for healing and deliverance. Some individuals appeared to be checked out altogether as they received deep spiritual healing from bitterness, anger, or abuse. Still, others left the room in distress because they were unable to accept that the presence in that place was the Spirit of God, offended as they were in the active spiritual atmosphere. I can best describe the experience of that meeting to be like living in a chapter from the Book of Acts. There were beautiful encounters with Jesus taking place, and there was evidence of The Holy Spirit that included signs, wonders, and miracles.

Have you ever been in a place that was rich with the presence of God? This may have been in a church or at a concert, while watching a movie, listening to a speaker, or just alone by yourself reading the Bible. Perhaps it was in a dream or while quietly lying in bed. If you have experienced the closeness of God's presence at many times (or any time in your life), you may have thought to yourself, "I feel completely satisfied, and I have no desire at all to sin or leave the presence of God." When you are in the atmosphere of God's presence, your desires change.

The atmosphere that we walk into affects us, just as surely as we can affect the atmosphere that we walk into.

It could be minutes later, hours later, maybe even days later before temptation gets put in front of you and all of a sudden you feel your desires beginning to change once again. If you follow whatever temptation you are facing today, you will know in your spirit that you have fallen short of Yahweh's glory and holiness.

One of the largest challenges that some believers in Yahweh face is that when they leave the atmosphere of His presence, they encounter the power of the air and face a strong shift in the atmosphere toward temptation. But the secret of holiness, which we will discuss further, is that you can steward and cultivate the atmosphere of The Holy Spirit at all times because He lives *inside* each person who believes in Jesus, while the atmosphere of the power of the air is *outside* of a person.

Apart from your own free will and decision to sin (I'm not taking any responsibility away from you as an individual who has made sinful choices), it is because the atmosphere changes around you that you stumble and fall. It is because your flesh is literally at war with your spirit (breath) within you. Whatever you therefore choose to fill your atmosphere with affects the decisions that you decide to make because of the power at work in the air. This is why the message of a simple children's song is so potently powerful and true. "Be careful, little eyes, what you see; be careful, little ears, what you hear . . ." The things you surround yourself with, the atmospheres you cultivate, become life or death to your spiritual walk.

But what about the atmospheres created by others?

You enter into a cafe and hear words of accusation and anger flowing out of a customer's mouth. He is making a great effort, with the help of expletives, to explain how the barista made a mistake with the order, and now he wants his money back. It starts subtly enough, with only the next customer in line within earshot. She looks awkwardly at her phone, trying at first to avoid eye contact with the barista, believing this will nullify the embarrassment. The level of aggression increases, suggesting to the newlywed couple who just walked through the door that the incident is significant. Hearing the shouts, they turn around and exit the building; after all, there's another coffee shop across the street. Meanwhile, the angry customer has just taken things up another level, slamming the coffee cup on the counter, sending a splash of hot java toward the register. They're going all in. The sad thing is, the drink he's purchased only cost three dollars and fifty cents. Everyone within earshot interprets the response of this customer to be, for lack of better words, sinful. No matter what the staff and other customers' reactions are, every soul in that place has just entered into the angry person's atmosphere. His sphere of influence has begun to affect each person in one way or another. While a few shrug it off and move on, for some the ripple effect sours their next phone call or meeting. For others, when they finally get home after a full day of tasks, meetings, and errands, they feel more tired and agitated than normal. They've blended the morning's events at the cafe with everything else they've experienced during the day. They lost their peace of mind for an entire day as a result of two minutes of "bad coffee."

The definition of *atmosphere* helps us understand what impact Satan has had on the air that surrounds us. *Atmosphere* is defined as "the pervading tone or mood of a place or situation."[8] It is also defined as "the air in any particular place."[9] *Air* is defined as "the invisible gaseous substance surrounding the earth." Sin and darkness make a lot more sense when you think of them in this context. Ephesians 6:12 (KJV) says, "For we wrestle not against flesh and blood, but against principalities, against powers, against the rulers of the darkness of this world, against spiritual wickedness in high places."

My brothers and I create films through our company called Unveil Studios. In 2015, we were in Thailand in production on our film called *She Has A Name*.

---

8 Lexico, s.v. "atmosphere," accessed May 8, 2020, https://www.lexico.com/en/definition/atmosphere

9 Lexico, s.v. "air," accessed May 8, 2020, https://www.lexico.com/en/definition/air

As I mentioned earlier, the movie is based on a real human trafficking event. We were filming scenes in the daytime on location in an actual "gogo bar" that had been investigated and temporarily shut down for sex trafficking of minors. We had a cast and crew that typically got along swimmingly because we shared the same vision, which was to complete the film together with excellence. However, we encountered all kinds of problems this particular day. Not equipment or technical issues (although I'm sure we had those too), but human nature problems. Sin problems. The atmosphere was affecting certain people in a very obvious way. What I mean by that is some of the people who were stable for days or even weeks before this production day began acting out in various ways. Some of the cast and crew walked off the set temporarily. A loud argument erupted, and the other people in their department were all thinking, "What they're arguing about is not a big deal." Another head of department threatened to quit and disappeared for several hours. A negative energy emerged on parts of the set. This was more than a typical angst associated with deadlines and creative perspectives. What I'm talking about was an actual atmosphere and presence at work in that place.

Sometimes a specific person will simply come near you, and you feel a shift in the atmosphere. Sometimes the way that someone speaks makes you feel slimy or gross. Many if not all of us know someone who speaks words that are just plain lacking in hope or joy. There is an atmosphere in the air around us, and it impacts each of the people around us.

Do you have a responsibility to act in holiness when the sin and darkness of others enters your atmosphere? According to the Bible, the answer is a resounding *yes*. Remember the story of Lot and his family, surrounded as they were every day by vile corruption and sin? The righteous Yahweh actually sent angels to rescue Lot from the corruption surrounding his family, but the ones who chose to hold on to the sinful desires of their dwelling place in Sodom and Gomorrah were destroyed.

> "For if God did not spare angels when they sinned, but sent
> them to hell, putting them in chains of darkness to be held
> for judgment; if he did not spare the ancient world when he
> brought the flood on its ungodly people, but protected Noah, a
> preacher of righteousness, and seven others; if he condemned
> the cities of Sodom and Gomorrah by burning them to ashes,
> and made them an example of what is going to happen to the
> ungodly . . ." (2 Pet. 2:4–6 NIV)

If you breathe in the spirit of this age, you'll breathe out malice, fear, contempt, jealousy, bitterness, brokenness, regret, anger, and the many other manifestations at work in the air in our present atmosphere. The breath of the spirit in the air will ultimately lead to death.

What air or atmosphere are you breathing in? Because what you breathe in will change what you breathe out. If you breathe in the Spirit of life and holiness, you will breathe out that same Spirit. You'll breathe out words of peace and hope. You'll breathe out emotions of joy and thanksgiving. You'll breathe out the fruit of the spirit—love, joy, peace, patience, kindness, goodness, gentleness, self-control.

There are two different kingdoms at work in our world, and these two kingdoms bear different kinds of fruit. The fruit of the two kingdoms is completely different because the source of a life's fruit depends on the cultivation and care that a person gives to their heart. The heart is a person's spiritual center. What a person breathes in will either become a breath of the Spirit of life and holiness or a breath of the spirit of this world and this dark age.

Ephesians 2:1–3 (NKJV) says, "And you *He made alive*, who were dead in trespasses and sins, in which you once walked according to the course of this world, according to the prince of the *power of the air, the spirit* who now works in the sons of disobedience, among whom also we all once conducted ourselves in the lusts of our flesh, fulfilling the desires of the flesh and of the mind, and were by nature children of wrath, just as the others."

According to this Scripture, Satan is a spirit as well. Notice the symbolism and wordplay in this. It says, "YOU, HE MADE ALIVE," like when Yahweh breathed on Adam in the Garden of Eden. Then it says, "but the spirit of this world," or the breath of this world, who is in the *air*, is at work. In this verse we find a secret about the world and strategies of the enemy, Satan. He has polluted the spiritual atmosphere and, by extension, the physical atmosphere or air. You could say that the lungs of the planet are infected, and by inhaling the air, the infection has spread from the lungs into the heart and become distributed throughout the body.

It is, after all, your lungs that collect oxygen from the air, moving oxygen into your heart, which pumps oxygenated blood throughout your body. What a person breathes in, moves first into their heart and then from their heart into their entire body.

Jeremiah 17:9 (NLT) says, "The human heart is the most deceitful of all things, and desperately wicked. Who really knows how bad it is?"

Mark 7:21 (BSB) says, "For from within the hearts of men come evil thoughts, sexual immorality, theft, murder, adultery."

Yahweh knows this corruption, and in the early years of His creation, He was grieved in His own heart that He made humanity. From the first sibling rivalry that resulted in Cain murdering Abel, to the millions of sins and rebellions that followed. Satan knows that he has the power to corrupt humanity, because he has infected the atmosphere.

At the time of this writing in early 2020, the novel coronavirus (COVID-19) has been declared a pandemic by the World Health Organization. It has forced closures of millions of businesses, governments have enforced lockdowns in many countries, and social distancing or isolation is in place for over three billion people internationally. Public places are shut down, and organizations and charities are canceling events up to six months in advance. The Olympics, which my wife and I essentially practice social distancing for two weeks to watch every two years, has been canceled.

The reason behind the global effort is that the virus is a communicable infection believed to be passable from one person to as many as a dozen others, perhaps more. This means that an exponential increase of infections can happen in a short amount of time. Measles was known to spread from one person to up to eighteen others. Until COVID-19 there has never been such a worldwide impact or global effort to curb infection of a virus, or the technology and communication measures available to attempt to do so. It's not yet known how damaging this particular virus will be, but at the time of this writing, it's infected around 400,000 people, causing an estimated 16,000 deaths.

Beyond the practical impact on world economies and the day-to-day lives of the majority of people on the planet, you could say that one particular emotion seems to get more coverage in the media and in conversations than any other: fear. Fear sells news subscriptions and releases chemicals in the brain that keep people coming back for more.

Sin is a virus that infects not only the body, but also the spirit. The infection of sin has spread worse than every other virus on the earth combined and infected every single person ever. Except for One. And sin is ultimately lethal in every single human case ever. Except for One. That is a horribly infected, contagious atmosphere.

Paul the apostle spoke about his concern that Christians in Corinth were easily led astray and tempted by different "spirits" from the One, Jesus, they had received. What's alarming is that the temptation is real enough to deceive even followers of Christ, who at one time willingly received Him. Paul even compares the deception of believers to the deception of Eve, another parallel from Genesis to present day.

> "I am afraid, however, that just as Eve was deceived by the serpent's cunning, your minds may be led astray from your simple and pure devotion to Christ. For if someone comes and proclaims a Jesus other than the One we proclaimed, *or if you receive a different spirit than the One you received*, or a different gospel than the one you accepted, you put up with it way too easily." (2 Cor. 11:3 BSB, emphasis added)

Even believers are putting up with deception way too easily. If you want to keep breathing the right Spirit, *Yahweh's Spirit*, then you have to clear the air. You have to move the spirit of the air out. In order to deal with the polluting demonic forces in the air, you have to first become aware they are at work. Then you have to actively operate in the power of The Holy Spirit to change the atmosphere. Thankfully, we have numerous examples of this in Scripture, along with stories from other followers of Jesus that exemplify it.

I became aware of another influence in our present atmosphere in the lead up to a recent mission trip to Thailand. Before we departed, I was asking Yahweh for a word for our team. This was the same thing I did before the Tanzania mission when the Lord gave me the word *breath*. This time around, I was asking Yahweh about Thailand, thinking about the missionaries our team would be visiting.

Suddenly, I heard a word very clearly: "Bestow."

I became excited about this word because I believe the purpose of short-term missions is to encourage and strengthen long-term missionaries. Statistics show a majority of missionaries are either burning out or burnt out in the mission field. While we were venturing out on a short-term mission to do good works, these long-term missionaries were in the trenches every day on the front lines.

While in Chiang Mai, Thailand, we met with some missionaries from British Columbia, Canada, who have operated a counselling center there for more than six years. They have fifteen full-time staff members who counsel missionary families, and their facility is full all the time. Our friend shared that over 80 percent of the missionaries they counsel are there for healing or support because of burnout while in the mission field.

People often wrestle with their conscience on short-term missions because they say they want to do something really practical, really meaningful. They want to get a lot done. But I've discovered that on a short-term mission, we actually go to carry and alleviate our brothers' and sisters' burdens, not to get a lot of "work done." We have the opportunity to bestow a blessing of encouragement on every single person we meet, but especially on those who serve.

Under the heading "Carrying Each Other's Burdens," Galatians 6:9–10 (BSB) says, "Let us not grow weary in well-doing, for in due time we will reap a harvest, if we do not give up. Therefore, as we have opportunity, let us do good to everyone, and especially to the family of faith."

The concept is simple. If you're serving the Lord (Yahweh), there is an enemy who makes it his goal to try and discourage and disrupt your work because the good that you're doing poses a serious threat to his kingdom.

We made a point of prophesying and praying over each staff person and missionary we met in Thailand, and one after the other, they shared about how much of a gift this was to them. Many came out of these group prayer times with tears and testimonies or looking visibly lighter. These were prayer times infused with the life-breathing power of The Holy Spirit.

One of the many highlights for me was seeing our dear friend, a seventy-five-year-old abolitionist working to pull women and girls from the red-light districts of Thailand. She is one of my heroes. She was in tears as she shared how we had bestowed on her a blessing, a will to carry on, an encouragement, a gift. A breath of life, if you will. And that is exactly why we had come. There were numerous times like this on our trip, and they were the highlight and purpose of our time in Thailand.

Between this experience in Thailand and numerous recent stories from friends and family, it's become clear that one of the main areas the enemy is attacking right now, whether in your day-to-day life or overseas in the mission field, is the area of *anxiety*. Sometimes you just hear or say the word and your heart rate changes.

According to the American Psychology Association, anxiety is an emotion characterized by feelings of tension, worried thoughts, and physical changes, such as increased blood pressure. [10] People with anxiety disorders usually have recurring intrusive thoughts or concerns. They may avoid certain situations out of worry.

Remember, the name of God, Yahweh, is on our very breath. Yahweh is meant to be our oxygen. But we have an enemy too, and he is called the "prince of the power of the air." He has corrupted and violated and permeated our atmosphere. His strategy is to manipulate human beings who let his atmosphere control or influence them. Since air is made up of particles, you could say that

---

10 "Anxiety," American Psychological Association, accessed May 8, 2020, https://www.apa.org/topics/anxiety/

if some of the particles of Yahweh are peace, hope, and joy, then the particles of Satan's atmosphere would be things like fear, bitterness, and anxiety. Anxiety is one of the major issues on the rise today because it is permeating our atmosphere. Thankfully, there is an antidote to the fear and the spirit of this world:

> "Cast all your anxiety on Him, because He cares for you. Be sober-minded and alert. Your adversary the devil prowls around like a roaring lion, seeking someone to devour. Resist him, standing firm in your faith and in the knowledge that your brothers throughout the world are undergoing the same kinds of suffering." (1 Pet. 5:7–9 BSB)

As indicated by our brothers and sisters being persecuted overseas, or by the burnout and anxiety of the missionaries in the mission field, the apostle Peter is still as right today as when he wrote this about two thousand years ago. Our brothers and sisters face the same kinds of suffering all around the world.

When a person is anxious or fearful, sometimes you can actually see it on them. It may be visibly on them, or you might not see it physically, but you definitely feel its presence. Many people wear their fears, anxieties, stresses, and burdens like a crown on their head. The burdens and fears in the kingdom of this world are a heavy and tarnished crown to wear.

But the Kingdom of Yahweh has been bestowed on all believers through Jesus Christ and The Holy Spirit.

One of the truly inspiring parts of the ministry of Jesus is found in his deliverance ministry. There are examples of men, women, and children whom Jesus sets free from being overtaken and possessed by evil spirits. Yahshua, meaning "Yahweh saves," delivers them from the oppression of the atmosphere of this world. He invites them into His Kingdom and transforms their lives, sometimes with as little as a word—in one breath.

"When they came to the crowd, a man approached Jesus and knelt before him. 'Lord, have mercy on my son,' he said. 'He has seizures and is suffering greatly. He often falls into the fire or into the water. I brought him to your disciples, but they could not heal him.' 'You unbelieving and perverse generation,' Jesus replied, 'how long shall I stay with you? How long shall I put up with you? Bring the boy here to me.' Jesus rebuked the demon, and it came out of the boy, and he was healed at that moment. Then the disciples came to Jesus in private and asked, 'Why couldn't we drive it out?' He replied, 'Because you have so little faith. Truly I tell you, if you have faith as small as a mustard seed, you can say to this mountain, 'Move from here to there,' and it will move. Nothing will be impossible for you.'" (Matt. 17:1–21 NIV)

The deliverance of a person from darkness into light is the ultimate calling of Jesus' followers. We are called to continue in Jesus' ministry, bringing His light to the world.

But the natural man, breathing in our natural atmosphere, is unable to discern the Spirit of God, let alone operate in the Spirit rather than the flesh.

"The person without the Spirit does not accept the things that come from the Spirit of God but considers them foolishness, and cannot understand them because they are discerned only through the Spirit." (1 Cor. 2:14 NIV)

In other words, the natural man, breathing in the natural atmosphere, is unable to discern. That is how corrupted the atmosphere is. The atmosphere is so toxic that people are unconscious of its toxicity. It's like carbon monoxide—a silent, invisible, and odourless killer. And no wonder there is such blindness, since the powers of this age have been around since ancient times and are experts at leading people astray and hiding themselves whenever it is most convenient to deceive.

You arrive at the office. The typical view of your fellow employees working away with their heads down has been interrupted. Nobody is making phone calls or typing emails. There seems to be a heaviness in the air and an unnatural silence. A private meeting between leadership and a particular employee in the board room has just ended. A door slams, and that employee shuffles toward his cubicle for the last time to pack up his desk. Despite a lack of information, various employees begin choosing sides. Some automatically assume the employee did something horribly wrong, while others take the side of the employee and begin to feel embittered or distrusting of the management team and ownership. Once the fired employee leaves, the remaining staff get back to work. But for the rest of that day and even the next week, productivity is significantly depleted. Negativity seems to find its way into almost every water cooler conversation, regardless of the topic. The atmosphere of your place of work has been infected with fear, doubt, and many other emotions.

I love one of the basic tenets of Rick Joyner's ministry called Morning Star. He says that "it is a basic military principle that you cannot defeat an enemy that you cannot see." So, in a physical context the enemy, Satan, would appear to have a pretty massive advantage. The author of Ephesians says they are "spirits of wickedness in high places," (Ephesians 6:12 WEB) but as followers of Jesus we know that we are seated in a much higher place.

> "For he raised us from the dead along with Christ and seated
> us with him in the heavenly realms because we are united with
> Christ Jesus." (Eph. 2:6 NLT)

How can we see through the Spirit? We need to ask Yahweh for eyes to see. We all know that we have physical eyes, but there are eyes in our spiritual beings as well. We have to learn to rely on promptings, direction, and guidance from Ruach Elohim in order to discern what is happening in the spiritual atmosphere.

This includes very practical things, such as growing in your awareness to the emotions in the air. There are signals and triggers that you will begin to see in the people and places around you. When you become fine-tuned, you will notice them in your own mind and body and personal emotions as well. Since the atmosphere is the pervading tone or mood of the place or situation you are in, your desire should be to bring the atmosphere of Yahweh into the places and people that you find yourself with.

Practice assessing the atmosphere *before* responding to it. The reactionary or emotional responses of the flesh are not what your atmosphere needs. Your atmosphere needs an awareness and surrender to the Spirit of God.

One of the most practical tools that Jesus gave to His own followers for seeing Yahweh's Kingdom come was the Lord's Prayer. We are simply invited to ask Him to bring the atmosphere of Heaven down by translating it to earth. "Thy Kingdom come, Thy will be done. On earth as it is in Heaven."

We must also gain more and more discernment, because another deceptive tactic of Satan is to mimic the work of Yahweh in order to deceive people through the trickery of similarity. One of the final abominations of Satan finds him breathing new life into the image of the beast as a counterfeit of the neshawmaw breath of Yahweh into Adam.

> "The second beast was given power to *give breath to the image*
> of the first beast, so that the image could speak and cause all
> who refused to worship the image to be killed." (Rev. 13:15
> NIV, emphasis added)

Isn't that something? The devil actually mimics the First Breath of Yahweh that happened in the Garden of Eden. Blasphemy has rarely looked so blatant. The works of the devil are blasphemy against Yahweh, and the beast or the devil is even covered in blasphemous names that make him out to appear to bear the namesakes of the Godhead in order to deceive his followers.

It's time for the followers of Jesus to awaken and arise to our rightful place. While the ultimate calling is to rejoice that one's name is found in the Book of Life, one of the practical calls on all believers in Yahweh is to bring freedom to the captives under the power of this atmosphere, in the name of Jesus. The calling is to preach the Gospel of the Kingdom to all people, even to the ends of the earth. With the preaching of Christ comes the manifestation of the demonic forces that are losing hold of this world, and part of the work of the believer is to silence and cast down the influences, voices, and clutches of Satan in our world and present atmosphere.

Revelation 12:9–10 (BSB) says, "And the great dragon was hurled down, that ancient serpent called the devil and Satan, the deceiver of the whole world. He was hurled to the earth, and his angels with him. And I heard a loud voice saying in heaven, 'Now is come salvation, and strength, and the kingdom of our God, and the power of his Christ: for the accuser of our brethren is cast down, which accused them before our God day and night.'"

The ultimate defeat of Satan is depicted clearly in Revelation. We have a sure victory over the enemy, who is singlehandedly named the deceiver of the entire world. He has minions and forces at his command and has been a liar and deceiver from the very beginning. But he has been defeated by King Jesus once and for all. The prophetic reality of his defeat is already at work, which is why Jesus clearly taught His disciples, including those of us who are following Him today, to trample on and defeat the snakes and scorpions that we face in our lives.

The sad truth is that Adam, the first Adam from the Garden of Eden, breathed in the atmosphere of Satan and, instead of resisting, let Satan suck the holy oxygen right out of him. In so doing, Adam and Eve corrupted their spirits, the spirit of the breath of life of Yahweh. Adam and Eve agreed with Satan, and the neshawmaw breath of life was corrupted. This was the moment sin entered humanity. In this moment, sin became part of the DNA of humanity, and despite mankind's countless attempts at correcting his own course, whether by religion and works or human effort, it pleased Yahweh that apart from His Son Jesus there would never be any other remedy or Way.

And that is why we need the Second Breath.

CHAPTER 5

THE SECOND BREATH

"None of the rulers of this age understood it. For if they had, they would not have crucified the Lord of glory. Rather, as it is written: 'No eye has seen, no ear has heard, no heart has imagined, what God has prepared for those who love Him.' But God has revealed it to us by the Spirit. The Spirit searches all things, even the deep things of God."

— 1 Corinthians 2:8–10 BSB

I remember my mom describing the death of my beloved grandma. She was a matriarch in our family who represented faith and service, the power of prayer, and a lifestyle committed to Jesus. After a wonderful, long life, she passed away on my birthday, which helps me remember her every year.

My mom had called her sister during my birthday party to see how things were going with Grandma, who had been in the hospital for a few days. During the call, my mom learned her condition was progressing quickly, so she immediately booked a flight, boarded a plane, alerted the rest of her siblings en route, and arrived at the hospital just a few hours later. While the party at my house was coming to an end, my mom had already arrived by Grandma's side in time for my mom and her siblings to miraculously share their final words to her and shed tears together. With shallow breaths, and unable to move or communicate verbally, Grandma squeezed the hand of her oldest son, and then it happened—my dear grandma breathed her last. She had held on as my mom traveled by air from one province to another. As my mom so vividly described to us later, at the moment Grandma breathed her last, it was as if you could physically see her spirit leave her body. Not that a vapour was necessarily visible in the room, but the presence of Grandma was gone. Her body, the shell that once held her spirit, remained, but it was no longer filled with life. It was only a shell, as was Adam before the neshawmaw entered his being. Grandma was actually gone. As she exhaled her final earthly utterance of the name of her Creator with her last "YAH . . . WEH," her spirit left her body. And as a family of believers, we knew exactly where her spirit had gone. It had gone back to Yahweh, who gave her breath.

While I was working on this chapter, as if to drive the point home even more clearly to me, my wife's grandma, affectionately known as "Baba," passed away. I got the call from my wife explaining that any available family members would have a few moments to share our last words with Baba. A European immigrant with five children, Baba was a champion of the faith and will abide comfortably in the great cloud of witnesses. She committed her time and her heart to Jesus time and time again. Even up to her final days, she regularly shared the truth of the Gospel with people in her elder care home. She prayed day and night, night and day, for her children, grandchildren, relatives, and perfect strangers. And while I was writing about breath, in particular about our last breath returning our spirit to Yahweh, she too breathed her last.

We found out something incredible in the final hours when we were speaking words of love, thankfulness, and honour over Baba. Because of a brain bleed, Baba was in a comatose state and her body was not responding to any stimuli. Her reflexes and responses were gone; all of her senses were shutting down, but she was still breathing. In her condition, the doctor explained that the final sense to shut down is a person's hearing. Although we couldn't be certain she was comprehending our words, the doctor said that most likely she could still hear us speaking to her. We were only able to faintly imagine the things she was seeing while we thanked her for being a hero of the faith, setting an example for us, teaching us how to follow Jesus. We were also speaking words like Stephen the martyr and Christ on the cross, committing her spirit back into the hands of the Potter, asking the Father to receive back her neshawmaw breath of life, which had formed her life and shaped Baba's destiny. Meanwhile, she was likely seeing things that we have not yet comprehended as her spirit began the passage from this realm into eternity.

Another incredible thing happened. Her living son and middle daughter were not in the room at first, but two of her daughters were there. They told her that her other children were on an airplane, coming to share a few final moments with her. She held on all through the next day while her son and daughter made their way to the hospital from another province in the country. She had seemed to stop breathing several times already and remained unresponsive, but she fought all the more, waiting for all four children to be in the room with her. The two siblings finally arrived in time to share ten final minutes together with their mom. My wife, mother-in-law, and our two-year-old daughter (Baba's only great-granddaughter) joined in over a video call, and we all witnessed her last breath. They said her mouth couldn't move, that her body was incapable of any response, but with her four living children around her bed and the voice of her great-granddaughter saying, "Hi, Baba," over the airwaves, we all saw Baba begin moving her mouth for the first time in three days, as if to speak. Her cheeks rose, her face moved, and she smiled. Then at last, surrounded by affectionate family, she breathed her last. Very shortly after her last breath, a doctor pronounced that she had died, and Dennis, my father-in-law, emphatically stated, "She is gone, her body is still here, but she has gone to be with Jesus." The siblings in the room all agreed; there was a body in front of them, but her spirit and life force was no longer there.

My wife, Christy, and I found it amazing that as the functions and senses of a human body wind down, a person's hearing is the last thing to go. In other words, even a lost soul could hear and bear witness to the Gospel of the Kingdom with their final breaths. What a picture of Yahweh's grace. Yahweh Who Saves.

Indeed, Yahweh does save, and He specifically embedded His desire to save us in the name of our Savior, which carries a heavier weight when we use His name, "Yahshua," the name given to Him by Yahweh. Yahshua is the original Hebrew name for Jesus, made up of the short form of Yahweh's name, YAH, combined with "who saves" or "is salvation." So when we declare Jesus' name as Yahshua, we are literally saying, "Yahweh is Salvation" or "Yahweh Saves." I have begun practicing the declaration of Jesus' name as Yahshua, using the sound of my breath to speak the truth that Yahweh is my Savior.

Two incredible claims of Yahshua were "I and the Father are one" and "I came in My Father's name." The actual name of Yahweh (YAH) being present in our Savior's name, Yahshua, helps me recognize more directly that the Father and Son are One.[11]

We all experience the importance of names every day. If your name is Daniel (like mine) and a person calls out "David," you don't respond. My parents are two of my living heroes in life and leaders in the faith. That being said, they had four boys, and we were not always called by our proper names. For the purpose of a real-life example, and with only love for them, here is what I mean: As their youngest, sometimes I was called by the names of my siblings, starting with the oldest. The call started with "Christopher, Andrew, Matthew . . . Daniel." A personal low came during the few years we had a pet named Hobbes in our house. During that period of time, I was occasionally accidentally called by our dog's name—"Hobbes!" The point is, when you call someone by the wrong name, it lacks effectiveness. Although I was usually aware I was being called on, there was an obvious relational intimacy missing in these few moments as well (the majority of the time they got my name right). Our all-knowing Father knows when we are calling on Him. But there is an intimacy and connectedness that comes from knowing His true name. In the same way that there is a personal

---

11 There are whole books that could be written about why translators and transliterators of the biblical text changed the name of Yahshua to what Christians most commonly use today when referring to the Savior of the world, which is "Jesus." The short version behind this metamorphosis from "Yahshua" to "Jesus" is that initially some of the authors believed the name of Yahweh was too holy to pronounce. So, the Yah sounds were emphasized in some translations differently so that readers would pronounce His name with a Ye sound rather than Yah. Next the Greek and then Latin languages came along with the introduction of the J sound. This is the same reason why "Yahweh" morphed into "Yehovah" before becoming most commonly translated as "Jehovah." Over the course of time and through various translations, "Jesus" emerged. The more accurate English translation would be "Joshua," which also means "Yahweh is salvation." However, in hopes of connecting readers more directly to the true name of our Savior, rather than translating His name into English, throughout the remainder of this book the name of Jesus will be written as Yahshua, the name given to Him by His Father Yahweh.

connection to our Father and breath of life when we call upon His name as Yahweh, the same applies to the name of our Savior.

Yahshua is the proper name of our Savior, because that is the name Yahweh declared to Mary and Joseph as His name. And how much more important in this case, since Yahshua is the "name above all names" (Phil. 2:9).

The First Breath that shaped humanity came from Yahweh in the Garden of Eden in between the tree of life and the tree of the knowledge of good and evil. It was a breath given in holiness in the presence of two different kingdoms. Its power made the first Adam come alive. But the Second Breath that shaped humanity came from the lungs of Yahshua at the cross, where He was crucified on a tree. The Second Breath that shaped humanity was an exhale. The neshawmaw received by Adam in Eden was humanity's First Breath and an inhaled "breath of life." The Second Breath was an exhaled breath by Yahshua that could be labeled "the breath of death."

Imagine the cross as the intersection of the two trees in the Garden of Eden. Imagine that the horizontal line represents the tree of the knowledge of good and evil and the kingdom of this world, while the vertical line represents the path to life. The vertical plank of the cross was, however, pointing to the crowned King of the universe and the sign that Pilate hung upon the cross in Matthew 27:37 (NKJV): "And they put up over His head the accusation written against Him: THIS IS JESUS [YAHSHUA] THE KING OF THE JEWS." His name, meaning "Yahweh Saves," was actually hung on His cross where His crime and punishment was clearly stated, "This is Salvation [Yahshua]." He was put to death for being our Savior and King.

Like every daughter or son of man before Him, the neshawmaw was with Yahshua at the cross. Profoundly, it was given back to Yahweh when Yahshua spoke His final words, recorded in Luke 23:46 (BSB, emphasis added): "Then Jesus [Yahshua] called out in a loud voice, *'Father, into Your hands I commit My Spirit.' And when He had said this, He breathed His last.*"

Remember that the connection between Yahweh and humanity came through the neshawmaw breath of life. Breath and spirit are interchangeable in the Old Testament word *ruach*. And in the New Testament, breath and spirit are interchangeable as well. The word *breath/spirit* in this verse comes from the

Greek word *pneuma*. Yahshua gives up His spirit, His breath, and in this same final exhale, He breathes his last.

The Second Breath, humanity's breath of death, was exhaled when the spirit of Yahshua was given up in his final breath.

In the Gospel accounts of Yahshua's death, Matthew, Mark, Luke, and John all describe the final exhale of Jesus as a man on behalf of sinful humanity. Interestingly, they all use similar phrasing:

"He gave up His spirit." (Matt. 27:50 NIV)

"With a loud cry, Jesus [Yahshua] breathed his last." (Mark 15:37 NIV)

"When he had said this, he breathed his last." (Luke 23:46b NIV)

"With that, he bowed his head and gave up his spirit." (John 19:30b NIV)

The Son of Man came as the Savior of humanity; His destiny written in His name, Yahshua, Yahweh Who Saves. Yahshua literally saved all who will believe in Him through the cross, while being found in the form of a man.

And you have to see that the final breath of Yahshua on the cross is the final exhale of Christ as a man who is the Second Adam.

Remember the first man (and son of God), Adam, inhaled the First Breath, the breath of life. And now, very specifically, the Gospels record how Jesus, who was Himself God, emptied Himself of His deity, becoming the Second Adam so that "Yahweh Who Saves" could redeem all of humanity by finishing the work of Yahweh and becoming the perfect sacrifice, once and for all on behalf of sinful humanity. Paul describes it perfectly in Hebrews 10:1–18 (ESV, emphasis added):

CHRIST'S SACRIFICE ONCE FOR ALL

"For since the law has but a shadow of the good things to come instead of the true form of these realities, it can never, by the same sacrifices that are continually offered every year, make perfect those who draw near. Otherwise, would they not have ceased to be offered, since the worshipers, having once been cleansed, would no longer have any consciousness of sins? But in these sacrifices there is a reminder of sins every year. For it is impossible for the blood of bulls and goats to take away sins. Consequently, when Christ came into the world, he said, 'Sacrifices and offerings you have not desired, but a body have you prepared for me; in burnt offerings and sin offerings you have taken no pleasure. Then I said, "Behold, I have come to do your will, O God, as it is written of me in the scroll of the book."' When he said above, 'You have neither desired nor taken pleasure in sacrifices and offerings and burnt offerings and sin offerings' (these are offered according to the law), then he added, 'Behold, I have come to do your will.' He does away with the first in order to establish the second. *And by that will we have been sanctified through the offering of the body of Jesus Christ once for all.* And every priest stands daily at his service, offering repeatedly the same sacrifices, which can never take away sins. But when Christ had offered for all time a single sacrifice for sins, he sat down at the right hand of God, waiting from that time until his enemies should be made a footstool for his feet. For by a single offering he has perfected for all time those who are being sanctified. And the *Holy Spirit also bears witness to us . . .*"

Now this amazes me. When you die as a human being and breathe your last breath on earth, your spirit actually goes out of your body with your last breath.

When the breath of life leaves your body, your spirit returns to Yahweh who gave it. After your spirit is gone, your physical body returns to the dust.

"And the dust returns to the ground it came from, and the spirit returns to God who gave it." (Eccles. 12:7 NIV)

Physiologically, within just a few hours of a person's death, the brain and organs begin to break down and liquefy. Within a few days the human body begins to decompose. Depending on the way that a body is buried, within five to ninety years the remaining shell of a human body, including all tissue and even the bones, will literally be entirely returned to dust. While the shell of a body remains for a while before it literally becomes dust, the spirit leaves the body at the moment of the last breath.

We see this moment of a spirit's passage to Yahweh highlighted again in Acts 7:59 (BSB): "While they were stoning him, Stephen appealed, 'Lord Jesus, receive my spirit.'"

Moments later, the great follower of Yahshua named Stephen became the first martyr. He was given a brief window into the Kingdom of Heaven, then he breathed his last. His spirit went to Yahshua (who is one with the Father Yahweh) into the presence of the same King he saw while he was dying.

> "And he said, 'Behold, I see the heavens opened, and the Son of Man [Yahshua] standing at the right hand of God [Yahweh].'" (Acts 7:56 ESV)

Similarly, as my grandma and my wife's Baba breathed their last breaths, their spirits returned to Yahweh, who gave them life. So it was with the Son of Man.

As Yahshua breathed His last, remember He also said, "It is finished." This means He actually finished Yahweh's work and brought it to completion, having lived a life without sin, in fellowship unbroken from His Father. The only man ever to live a life without a single breath of sin or blasphemy toward Yahweh.

While being found in the form of a man, Yahshua never once took Yahweh's name in vain, not even with a single breath!

Every breath of Yahshua is life, save His final exhale on the cross, which was a breath of death in the flesh. This was accomplished so that you and I could be crucified with our old being in Christ. Through His death and resurrection, Yahshua completed His work. The "it is finished" moment is one the fate of humanity hinges upon. The moment when Yahshua breathed out his last exhaled breath as a man, by exhaling His final "YAH . . . WEH" to the Father. And in that moment, all of humanity was given a Second Breath from Yahweh!

The identification of God throughout Scripture as Father, Son, and Holy Spirit is one of the great mysteries of God. Endless research, teaching, and study have gone into discerning Their mystery. Rather than break down the many facets of the relationship of *Ruach Elohim* (in Hebrew Ruach Elohim is plural, not singular), simply read the words of Yahshua and consider this incredible revelation about the relationship between Yahshua and Yahweh:

"I and the Father are one." (John 10:30 NIV)

Yahshua said, "I and the Father are one." So, the "YAH" or "Y-H" or "Yod-Hey" (inhaled breath from the Garden), which was breathed into Adam's nostrils, was a breath from Yahshua (Jesus) in the Garden of Eden just as much as it was a breath from Yahweh. And the last breath of Jesus, "WEH" or "W-H" or "Waw-Hey" that Yahshua exhaled at the cross, returned His spirit to Yahweh and restored the holy breath of God to humanity!

The First Breath brought us physical life. The Second Breath brought us redemption because it was breathed back in holiness to Yahweh. Yahweh Who Saves redeemed our corrupted breath when He died at the cross!

This is also why Yahshua (Jesus) is the First and the Last. The First Breath came from the Father Yahweh (who is one with the Son) in the Garden of Eden and entered into the lungs of the first Adam. Every breath from the time of the first Adam's sin until Yahshua was a corrupted breath, and because of man's sin, the spirit of man was separated from a Holy God . . . until the last breath on behalf of sinful humanity was breathed by God's grace *from the lungs of Yahshua, the Second Adam.*

What an incredibly weaved, intimate, and elaborate story! The breath of life moves from the Father Yahweh all the way through humanity, from Yahweh's first son, Adam, generation to generation, all the way to you and me. And in Yahshua, the Second Adam, it is returned to Yahweh so that redemption can be eternally established for all who believe!

Remember how breath can be a word? Like the whisper of Yahweh to Elijah in the desert? Like the quiet utterance of the name of Yahweh with our every breath? Rising and falling with every "YAH . . . WEH" as breath enters and leaves our physical bodies? Yahshua, the Alpha and Omega, gets the first word and He gets the last word. He is the Giver of Breath, Ruach Elohim taking the form of Yahweh in the Garden of Eden. And He is the Son of Man, Yahshua, Yahweh Who Saves, as He exhales the neshawmaw breath of life at the cross!

Yahshua reshaped the history of humanity as we know it when He died carrying the sin and darkness of the entire planet on His shoulders. But by dying and fulfilling His purpose without sin, Yahshua restored Yahweh's breath of life for you and for me. Because of His life and fulfilled destiny, Yahshua is the Breath of Life. When Yahshua breathed out the neshawmaw, the exhale of death for sinful man, Yahweh received the perfect sacrifice, poured out through Yahshua's blood at the cross. The neshawmaw was restored to what it was created to be once again (as we will see in the next chapter, it was actually more than simply restored, it was recreated). By living without sin, living a pure and holy life in the flesh as a man, by being the Son of God and Son of Man, uniting the Spirit with the body, Jesus restored the breath of Life for all who believe in him.

> "For by one sacrifice he has made perfect forever those who are being made holy." (Heb. 10:14 NIV)

When Yahshua breathed His Spirit back to Yahweh, He exhaled what humanity inhaled first in the Garden of Eden. The transfer between Father and Son was completely established forever. And the Son's next move was to bring this restored breath to humanity by giving us the Holy Breath itself.

CHAPTER 6

THE THIRD BREATH

"Ye have heard how I said unto you, I go away, and come again unto you. If ye loved me, ye would rejoice, because I said, I go unto the Father: for my Father is greater than I."

— John 14:28 KJV

There was notable tension in the atmosphere. Just like Ruach Elohim in Genesis 1, the Spirit of God hovers over the darkness and tension of creation. Fear has gripped the hearts of all Yahshua's disciples in Jerusalem, which is why they are hiding in an upper room afraid of the Jewish leaders. The Pharisees and teachers of the law aren't satisfied with the crucifixion of Yahshua; they want to bring a full reckoning to the move of God called the Way. Every known follower of Yahshua has become a target. Fear tangibly pollutes the air as the disciples breathe in the anxiety of the atmosphere. The gossip and energy brought on by the rumours of Christ's resurrection still overtake every shopkeeper and punctuate the conversations in the marketplace. A creak in the stairs. There must be someone behind the locked door. A presence can be felt approaching, coming with strange familiarity and unsettling doubt.

Suddenly, the impossible. A flash of light from the wall. A subtle vibration through the floor panels. Startled gasps and outbursts from the apostles. In a flash, a man who looks like Yahshua is standing among them, but somehow He emits a sweet fragrance, a glittering light, and immense power all at the same time. Before Peter can respond out of fear to silence the commotion, Yahshua takes over, "Peace be with you."

The greatest doubter of His small group of followers, Thomas, is not present as Yahshua draws back the robe overhanging His forearm. The holes that tore apart flesh and penetrated the bones in His wrist are there. He reveals the gaping holes in His feet where spikes almost an inch wide held those same feet to the cross. It is Yahshua. But He has a new body. Despite the open wounds on His hands and feet, there are no signs of blood or bruising. Wonder grips His followers. Indeed, a resurrected Jesus has just appeared in their midst.

Suddenly, the atmosphere changes. Fear melts into joy. Awe gives way to wonder, and wonder turns to worship. The human fear of man is overtaken by a reverent fear of Yahweh. More than one disciple remembers feeling this way before. It was on a boat on the Sea of Galilee. A sunny day abruptly turned into a furious attack on their livelihood. Seasoned fishermen, with great knowledge of the sea, were undone by this mysterious, raging storm. How could the atmosphere change so quickly? They felt the same fear in that boat as they felt in the upper room; only on that boat, Yahshua was with them when the storm began to rage, although asleep. So, they startled Him out of a dream, saying, "Lord, save us! We're going to drown." Yahshua arose then and rebuked the winds and waves *with a breath*. The hurricane-force winds and tumultuous waves were completely calm in a moment.

> "The men were amazed and asked, 'What kind of man is this?
> Even the winds and the waves obey him!'" (Matthew 8:27 NIV)

For the first time a few of the disciples actually knew the answer. As the centurion who crucified Yahshua testified, "Surely this man was the Son of God" (Mark 15:39 NIV). A man, yes, but now glorified, the disciples marveled at Him in amazement. The man they were following was about to fulfill the prophecies of Daniel, Joel, Ezekiel, John the Baptist, and many other prophets before them. Ruach Elohim, Yahweh, Yahshua was about to breathe.

But before the Third Breath of Yahweh can be given, we have to rewind to the moment it was established permanently. This moment in history was so monumental, that billions of people around the world have taken notice. It's also an incredible moment because every single denomination in Christianity actually agrees on its significance: *YAHSHUA ROSE FROM THE DEAD.*

Adrian Warnock outlines the significance of the resurrection in his book *Raised With Christ*, detailing the importance of history's most stunning moment. The following is a brief excerpt from his work:

> "Without their unwavering confidence in Jesus' resurrection, would the disciples have risked everything, and in many cases been killed, for their faith? People do die all the time for falsehoods that they themselves genuinely believe to be true. It is, however, impossible to believe that all of the disciples would die for something they knew to be a deliberate deception. The church did not create the resurrection stories; instead, the resurrection stories created the church."[12]

It's because of the resurrection that every believer is reintroduced to the life-giving force and power of Ruach Elohim. For it is through the resurrection that "the last Adam became a life-giving Spirit" (1 Cor. 15:45 ESV).

It does not say, "It is through the cross," but "through the resurrection that 'the last Adam became a life-giving spirit." Remember that His life-giving Spirit comes through His breath. It was through the cross that the final breath of humanity was breathed by Yahshua, and it was through the resurrection that Yahshua became a life-giving Spirit.

Yahshua was the first One in all creation to breathe in the Spirit that makes humanity a new creation. Therefore, He is able to exhale it upon His followers.

The cross is a necessity for all the world and all sinners in that Yahshua was poured out as our sacrifice by death at the cross. In other words, before we can receive new life, we have all been appointed first to die. And we were crucified with Christ (Gal. 2:20). Only after death can we experience resurrection.

---

12 Adrian Warnock, Raised with Christ: How the Resurrection Changes Everything (Wheaton, IL: Crossway, 2018).

The resurrection from the dead was the event that made Yahshua life-giving. In raising Him from the dead, Yahweh makes Yahshua the living proof of the resurrection of the dead. This event gives every believer anecdotal evidence of their own forthcoming resurrection after death. The resurrection is the reason the apostles and followers of Christ are called to be faithful even to death, because new life awaits beyond the grave.

Yahshua became the firstborn of many brothers and made a way for the earthly man to be transformed into the spiritual man.

> "So will it be with the resurrection of the dead. The body that is sown is perishable, it is raised imperishable; it is sown in dishonor, it is raised in glory; it is sown in weakness, it is raised in power; it is sown a natural body, it is raised a spiritual body. If there is a natural body, there is also a spiritual body. So it is written: 'The first man Adam became a living being'; the last Adam, a life-giving spirit. The spiritual did not come first, but the natural, and after that the spiritual. The first man was of the dust of the earth; the second man is of heaven. As was the earthly man, so are those who are of the earth; and as is the heavenly man, so also are those who are of heaven. And just as we have borne the image of the earthly man, so shall we bear the image of the heavenly man." (1 Cor. 15:42–49 NIV)

There is an immense poetry and purpose behind the delivery of the Third Breath. Yahshua knows how big the moment is, and I love how He plays it up with dramatic intensity. The delivery of the Third Breath harkens back to and resembles the First Breath in astounding ways. After all, Yahshua was in the First Breath that brought the First Adam to life in the Garden of Eden. He breathed out the Second Breath as the Second Adam at the cross. How fitting that He would bring dramatic emphasis while giving humanity our Third Breath.

And so the moment had come. Yahshua had calmed the storm again in the upper room, slicing through the atmosphere of fear and grief as He said, "Peace be with you. As the Father has sent me, I am sending you" (John 20:21 NIV).

In that moment the apostles recognized their Shepherd's voice. Then Yahshua paused. The moment of intention, "Yod." He inhales a deep breath, "Hey." He lets the breath fill His being and stir inside, "Waw." Then Yahshua breathes on the disciples, exhaling with the sound, "Hey." Y-H-W-H. Yod, Hey, Waw, Hey—the name of Yahweh on His breath. Then He said, "Receive the Holy Spirit [Ruach ha'Kodesh]."

Yahshua BREATHES out the life-giving Spirit as the Second Adam. This is the Third Breath.

> "On the evening of that first day of the week, when the disciples were together, with the doors locked for fear of the Jewish leaders, Jesus came and stood among them and said, 'Peace be with you!' After he said this, he showed them his hands and side. The disciples were overjoyed when they saw the Lord. Again Jesus said, 'Peace be with you! As the Father has sent me, I am sending you.' *And with that he breathed on them and said, 'Receive the Holy Spirit.* If you forgive anyone's sins, their sins are forgiven; if you do not forgive them, they are not forgiven.'" (John 20:19–23 NIV, emphasis added)

The Third Breath is my favorite breath of all, because its impact is the most monumental. While the First Breath of Yahweh in the Garden of Eden over Adam automated the *physical breath* of humanity, the Third Breath automates the *spiritual breath* of every saved believer. The Third Breath is a complete game changer and the fulfillment of hundreds of the most important prophecies throughout Scripture. A moment so incredible that Joel, Ezekiel, David, Moses, and Isaiah (the list goes on) all spoke about it!

One of the great mysteries of Yahweh's love is revealed powerfully through this Scripture. I believe the breath and life-giving Spirit of Jesus, which is shown here in the breathing and giving of The Holy Spirit, reveals to us the ultimate calling of Adam in the Garden of Eden and, by extension, the calling on you and I. *We are called to breathe life on people and to forgive sin.*

I don't understand how this truth is skimmed over by millions of believers, other than the simple reality that the prince of the power of the air does not want believers to understand it. Because it changes everything and has the power to change every soul on this earth. For Yahshua clearly says, "If you forgive anyone's sins, their sins are forgiven."

I guess one question that you can wrestle with personally is this: Did Yahshua really mean this when He said it?

You and I were created in the image of Yahweh to live out the ministry of Yahshua by the power of The Holy Spirit. God breathes into man so that man can breathe God's nature and love and presence into others.

Breathe that in for a moment. You were created in the image of Yahweh, according to Genesis 2:7. You were destined to continue the work of Yahshua, according to John 20:22. And you are enabled to actually do this supernatural work because of The Holy Spirit, according to Romans 8:11 (CEV), "Yet God raised Jesus to life! God's Spirit now lives in you, and he will raise you to life by his Spirit."

The Holy Spirit is the holy breath of life. The Third Breath, which is the final and farthest-reaching breath that shapes humanity, is not only the breath of life, it's the breath of eternal life. It is the breath of The Holy Spirit, in Hebrew *Ruach ha'Kodesh*, which means "The Set Apart Spirit."

I love that in this narrative, the breath or Spirit moves from the Father, to the Son, to The Holy Spirit. The complete unity of the Godhead: Father (Yahweh), Son (Yahshua), and Holy Spirit (Ruach ha'Kodesh) is clearly shown.

The Third Breath comes out of Yahshua's lungs once again, but this time the breath is from the resurrected Jesus Christ, who has literally conquered sin and death. Reminiscent of that moment in the Garden of Eden, Yahshua, the Second Adam, breathes His name, "YAH . . . WEH," over his disciples, and they receive their first redeemed breath from Yahweh on earth. Their spirits are given new life and the promise of an eternal life with the Creator of everything.

But when The Holy Spirit is breathed by Yahshua into the apostles, this is no longer Yahshua breathing as the Son of Man, but Yahshua as I AM, Yahshua as Yahweh, Yahshua as Ruach Elohim, the fullness of all things. Yahshua as All In All. Yahshua as First and Last. Yahshua as Isaiah called him: Mighty God and

Everlasting Father. This is everything—the restoration of the Spirit of holiness and the breath of life! The breath is restored to humanity once again like it was given in the Garden of Eden. But this time it's even better than the uncorrupted neshawmaw breath of life from Genesis. Adam and Eve traded in their life-giving breath and the indwelling Spirit of God when they sinned, but through Yahshua (Jesus Christ) the breath and Spirit of life is restored to all who believe. Whereas everyone breathing the neshawmaw is destined once to die, the breath of eternal life comes with the promise of resurrection!

The Third Breath is the moment of new creation!

The significance of Yahshua imparting Ruach ha'Kodesh through breath is paramount for understanding our connection to Yahweh in our daily lives. The entire purpose of this revelation is to ground us in the mystery of being made in His image, of receiving a physical and spiritual impartation from God Himself. The First Breath was the neshawmaw breath of life that made our physical bodies alive. The Third Breath is The Set Apart Spirit of God that seals every believer in Yahshua with the promise of resurrection life and an eternal life with our Creator. Both came from the "lungs" of Yahweh/Yahshua, and both came through the physical act of breathing upon humanity.

Once more, let me emphasize what the significance of breath is in this narrative. *Breath is the most inseparable characteristic of every living person!* Without your next breath, you will literally cease to physically exist. Without your next breath, you will return back to dust. But with your next breath, which is a form of uttering your Creator's name, you are repeating the moment of creation in Genesis 2:7 and the moment of new creation in John 20:22.

2 Corinthians 1:21b–22 (BSB) confirms this: "He anointed us, placed His seal on us, and put His Spirit [Ruach ha'Kodesh] in our hearts as a pledge of what is to come."

After the giving of the Holy Breath of Life in John 20, Jesus prepares the disciples for the most earth-shaking moment in our history besides the resurrection, the day of Pentecost. Why is it significant that the upper room narrative resembles the story of Genesis? Because the story of Genesis is the story of the corruptible man, humanity in the flesh, and the first creation. It's the story of the first Adam. John's Gospel tells us the story of the incorruptible man, humanity in the Spirit, and the new creation. It's the story of the Second Adam. We are being guided on a visual tour of the history of humanity by the Creator Himself.

The Second Breath was a breath of death on behalf of all humanity by Yahshua on the cross. Before you are raised to new life, in order to become a new creation you must first let the earthly man die! The breath of death at the cross made way for the Third Breath, which brings new creation life to the follower of Yahshua. It began when Yahshua breathed eternal life upon the disciples. At Pentecost, the breath of The Holy Spirit (Ruach ha'Kodesh) also came with power.

Yahshua specifically tells the disciples to wait until Ruach ha'Kodesh comes in power. They have an incredible message to share with the world, but up until Pentecost, they don't have the power they need to bring the good news about Yahshua to the world.

Why did Yahshua wait until after the resurrection to give Ruach ha'Kodesh to the disciples? After all, they were together day and night for at least a year during the active part of His ministry. The simple answer is that He was not yet able to! The Holy Spirit first had to bring Yahshua back to life as evidence of His perfect life and sacrifice! And now Yahshua, in resurrected glory, became a life-giving Spirit!

Because of the completed work of Yahshua at the cross, and most importantly through His resurrection from the tomb, we have been given free and living access to the Third Breath of Yahweh. This new breath is the breath of The Holy Spirit, and this is the breath of God that is available to all people, in all places, at all times if they receive Yahshua and are indwelled by the Set Apart Holy Spirit (Ruach ha'Kodesh).

The Word became flesh, inhaled the neshawmaw (the First Breath), and lived a life where every breath was breathed in communion with Yahweh. He exhaled the neshawmaw (the Second Breath) back to Yahweh, then breathed in the Ruach ha'Kodesh (the Third Breath), which is Yahweh's Set Apart Spirit that has the power, as evidenced in Yahshua, to transform the earthly man into the heavenly man.

What amazes me about the coming of Ruach ha'Kodesh (The Holy Spirit) is that the Spirit comes as a deposit into our very hearts, as Paul describes, or as other Scriptures say, into the hearts of every believer in Yahshua. The coming of the power of Yahweh is once again as a vital breath, an invisible force, a wind. The neshawmaw breath of life meant all these things to a degree as well. But Ruach ha'Kodesh differs because Ruach ha'Kodesh means "The Set Apart Spirit of God."

Each and every created human being has a spirit, or breath. But there is individuality in each of our spirits. However, The Holy Spirit comes as the uniting, all-powerful, Set Apart Spirit of Yahweh—the breath of eternal life for every believer and the deposit in the believer that guarantees resurrection from the dead. Every individual can invite Ruach ha'Kodesh (The Holy Spirit) in because of the finished work of Yahshua and be bound together in perfect unity. The Set Apart Spirit is the uniting power of God.

But don't mistake this uniting force as being singular in expression. Ruach ha'Kodesh distributes the gifts and power and wisdom of God creatively, taking into account the unique calling and destiny of every person who receives The Set Apart Spirit. It wouldn't be nearly as exciting or creative if we were all meant to become identical. Becoming one through the Spirit, we operate differently in body. Consider how creatively Yahweh made the earth, the universe, and mankind. The Spirit of God is immensely powerful and creative and life-giving, imparting gifts of prophecy, the fruit of the Spirit, hospitality and service, gifts like speaking in tongues and interpretation, practical, ministry, and teaching gifts, words of knowledge, and every spiritual blessing imaginable. They are all unique gifts and skills, and they all come through the work of One Spirit, Ruach ha'Kodesh, The Set Apart Holy Spirit of Yahweh.

"Are you not much more valuable than they?" (Matt. 6:26b NIV)

If you have any doubt about the unique calling and destiny on your life, consider the symbols Yahweh gives us in creation itself. Every snowflake that has ever fallen (or ever will) is unique (not to mention stunningly beautiful under a microscope). Every blade of grass that has ever grown is one of a kind (there is literally not one that is the same when they are studied under a microscope). Every branch and every flower and every seed and every cell has unique characteristics and individuality.

How much more, then, you and I, whom Yahweh calls His masterpiece! Yahweh the Potter is moulding and making you into an intricately shaped, beautifully stunning vessel of His presence!

The Third Breath of God that shapes humanity is an eternal deposit of life in everyone who believes. And better than that, it's a breath that comes with daily bread, in which we can find constant refreshment by breathing in the nature of Yahweh through the power of Ruach ha'Kodesh, The Holy Spirit, because of the finished work of Yahweh's Son, Yahshua.

My prayer is that you will invite the life-giving spirit of Yahshua (Jesus) into your heart and soul. The Set Apart Spirit, Ruach ha'Kodesh, will then abide in you and become your life-giving breath.

If you're like me, sometimes you have yearned for earlier times or looked back fondly on seasons of your life where you felt such a pure connection to Yahweh. The first memory I recall when I reflect on intimacy with God was when I first really experienced relationship with The Holy Spirit in my late teens and early twenties. I remember being so hungry for God's presence that I would lie down on the floor in my bedroom (actually, it was a living room with a curtain because that's what I could afford as a bachelor), and I would sob and cry out for God's presence, and Ruach ha'Kodesh would minister to the deep places of my soul. In that season of life, I didn't even need much sleep; I would sometimes sleep for only one or two hours a day, and I felt totally refreshed and invigorated. I was working a night shift at a grocery store and then working to develop my own business during daylight hours. But I wasn't tired. I was just hungry throughout the day to encounter Ruach ha'Kodesh.

I didn't have any of this revelation about the Breath of Life or many of the mysteries of God that I know today. I was simply a child encountering the King of the universe.

Whether you want to invite The Set Apart Spirit of God into your life today for the first time, or you already follow Yahshua and want a fresh breath of The Holy Spirit's life in your mind, body, and soul, I encourage you to breathe

Yahweh's Spirit in like never before. Let the practice of fellowshipping with The Holy Spirit become the new normal in your life.

Speak to Ruach ha'Kodesh as you would speak to your dearest friend. Take The Set Apart Spirit into your confidence by inviting the Spirit into your inner thoughts, hopes, dreams, and desires. I'm not speaking metaphorically. Literally ask, speaking out loud or in prayer, for Ruach ha'Kodesh to guide you and speak to you. Speak to God and share your secrets and make actual time to be alone with and consciously aware of Ruach ha'Kodesh. This can be as simple as finding a quiet place, free of distractions, where you can pray or talk to God and focus on The Holy Spirit.

Here is a simple exercise that makes you increasingly aware of Yahweh (YHWH) in your daily life:

First, find a quiet place where you will not be distracted. No phones or immediate interruptions.

Y – Step one: Begin to breathe, starting from that conscious pause of intention that takes place before you inhale, "Yod." Imagine Yahweh in the Garden of Eden. Before He breathed, He was looking at the face of Adam, but Adam was not yet alive. In the same way, imagine your own face, or one of your current circumstances or a person or any situation that needs to encounter Yahweh's breath, and experience His life-giving Spirit.

H – Step two: Breathe in, making the inhale sound "Hey." Shift your awareness entirely to Yahweh, your Giver of Breath. Imagine that you are not inhaling air, you are inhaling Ruach ha'Kodesh, The Set Apart Spirit.

W – Step three: "Waw." Before you exhale, pause to imagine The Holy Spirit indwelling your whole person. You're holding in the Holy Breath of Life, letting it infill your body, soul, and spirit.

H – Step four: "Hey." Exhale with faith or belief that you are breathing out the very Spirit of God. You are breathing new creation life into circumstances and situations in your life, over relationships, job opportunities, whatever you are focusing on.

The above process is a simple prayer exercise, infilled with a fine-tuned awareness of Yahweh and the power of His Breath of Life, which lives in you as a saved follower of Yahshua. If you become distracted by the timing of the four steps of the breath, simply become aware that Yahweh is your Breath of Life. And as you pray, know that you have been given power by Yahshua to breathe life over your circumstances by the power of Ruach ha'Kodesh, The Set Apart Holy Spirit of God. Become aware of your Creator's name as you pray and breathe. YAH . . . WEH. His name is on the sound of your every breath.

"You're closer than the breath I breathe."[13]

Another simple exercise: This can be done in any place, at any time. In fact, it's particularly effective in times of heightened stress, fear, or anxiety. This is a practical way to repeat the moment of creation and connect with God, who is in your every breath:

Whisper God's name or say it out loud: *Yahweh. Yahshua. Ruach ha'Kodesh. Father God. Jesus. Holy Spirit.*

As you become aware of His presence, thank Him for being your Life, your Breath, and your All in All. Let The Set Apart Spirit lead you into deeper fellowship. Let Him take you into the Garden. In that place of intimacy, because of Ruach Elohim's creativity, He will invite you into places that reveal His heart and love for you in powerful ways.

Simple exercises like these make your body and spirit more aware of the moment-by-moment presence of God! I believe as you practice spending *time* and dedicating yourself *purposefully* to Yahweh, in ways like these, you will enter into the greatest mystery of all creation: that you were created to have fellowship, daily bread, and daily communion with the Creator of the universe, because Almighty God designed you for intimacy and friendship with Him. That is what the story of Adam and Eve in the Garden of Eden was about before they rebelled against Him through sin, corrupting the purity of His Breath. Thankfully, His plan has always been to reconnect Himself with us. By His incredible love, He sent Yahshua so we can re-enter into that fellowship by the power of The Holy Spirit. Yahshua Himself tells us this.

---

13 Amanda Lindsey Cook, "Closer," released September 25, 2015, track 8 on Brave New World (Redding, CA: Bethel Music, compact disc).

"No longer do I call you servants, for a servant does not understand what his master is doing. But I have called you friends, because everything I have learned from My Father I have made known to you. You did not choose Me, but I chose you. And I appointed you to go and bear fruit—fruit that will remain—so that whatever you ask the Father in My name, He will give you. This is My command to you: Love one another." (John 15:15–17 BSB)

It's not time to shrink back or feel discouraged or breathe the anxiety, stress, and pollution in our atmosphere. It's time to move in The Set Apart Spirit, which is the opposite Spirit from the spirit that is in the world. It's time to reinvigorate your heart and soul through friendship with Yahweh, your very Breath of Life. Don't live in regret if today you feel far from the King. Look back with gratitude on the seasons of your life where you encountered the Father, Son, or Holy Spirit, and move forward with the certainty of friendship, knowing you are accepted as a son or daughter because Jesus Christ, Yahshua, has won your life and given you eternal breath by depositing His Ruach ha'Kodesh inside of you.

So often I think we play the same game of comparison in the Body of Christ as the world is playing in the media, social circles, and the proverbial rat race. But we are from a different Kingdom! We live for a future that is so incredible, the greatest saints couldn't describe its glory and even angels look into the mystery because of the unfathomable wonder: "And now this Good News has been announced to you by those who preached in the power of the Holy Spirit sent from heaven. It is all so wonderful that even the angels are eagerly watching these things happen" (1 Pet. 1:12 NLT).

Don't you want to be part of the story that even the angels of Heaven follow with eager anticipation? They are living in the very atmosphere of Almighty Yahweh, constantly before the throne of the resurrected and reigning Yahshua. Even so, they look into the mystery of this Good News!

I remember a word I got from Ruach ha'Kodesh recently, and I believe it is for every single man, woman, and child who is truly in friendship with Yahweh. It's an awesome call to purpose that should lead you to fear and trembling and seeking God daily, unless you should fall to pride and self-exaltation. "Arise. Shine. Your light has come."

This Word from God is found in Isaiah 60:1 (WEB), where the full verse states, "Arise, shine; for your light is come, and the glory of Yahweh is risen on you."

This is echoed again in Ephesians 5:14 (BSB): "So it is said: 'Wake up, O sleeper, rise up from the dead, and Christ [Yahshua] will shine on you.'"

It's time to walk together as one Body, filled with The Holy Spirit, breathing in a lifestyle of friendship with Yahweh.

> "Jesus answered, 'Very truly I tell you, no one can enter the
> kingdom of God unless they are born of water and the Spirit.
> Flesh gives birth to flesh, but the Spirit gives birth to Spirit.
> You should not be surprised at my saying, "You must be born
> again." The wind blows wherever it pleases. You hear its sound,
> but you cannot tell where it comes from or where it is going. So
> it is with everyone born of the Spirit.'" (John 3:5–8 NIV)

Here is an incredible truth: Ruach ha'Kodesh takes up residence inside of the saved believer. That means The Set Apart Spirit becomes a holy filter inside of you, bubbling up into overflowing rivers of life. This presence inside of you means The Set Apart Spirit can blow away the atmosphere of the air around you so that you live as a vessel of Yahweh's presence.

Isaiah spoke of this, saying to depart from evil and be separate; in effect, "It's time to be holy and set apart." He was seeing the revelation of the coming Ruach ha'Kodesh, who is the power inside every believer to be set apart (which literally means "holy"). Isaiah said through the Spirit, "Depart, depart, go out from there, touch no unclean thing! Go out of the midst of her! Cleanse yourselves, you who bear the vessels of Yahweh" (Isaiah 52:11 WEB). The vessels speak about the treasured *presence of Yahweh*, which refers to Ruach ha'Kodesh, Yahweh's Set Apart Spirit.

2 Corinthians 6:16–18 (KJV) expands on this: "And what agreement has the temple of God with idols? for you are the temple of the living God; as God has

said, I will dwell in them, and walk in them; and I will be their God, and they shall be my people. Therefore come out from among them, and be you separate, says the Lord, and touch not the unclean thing; and I will receive you, and will be a Father unto you, and you shall be my sons and daughters, says the Lord Almighty [Yahweh]."

One of the greatest Scriptures ever written for the saved believer holds a promise of immense value, explaining what will happen when we are living under the full-time influence of Ruach ha'Kodesh.

The words of Yahshua in John 7:38–41 (BSB): "Whoever believes in Me, as the Scripture has said: 'Streams of living water will flow from within him.' He was speaking about the Spirit, whom those who believed in Him were later to receive. For the Spirit had not yet been given, because Jesus [Yahshua] had not yet been glorified. On hearing these words, some of the people said, 'This is truly the Prophet.' Others declared, 'This is the Christ.'"

You cannot live a good life, let alone a set apart life, without Ruach ha'Kodesh. The mystery of the ages, revealed to us, is that the Spirit of Yahshua, who is Ruach ha'Kodesh, lives in those who believe. This is the same Spirit that raised Jesus from the dead! The same Spirit that hovered over the waters of a silent planet Earth and then exploded with creativity! The same Spirit that arrayed the heavens with galaxies innumerable! The same Spirit that gave breath to the first Adam and made the Second Adam a life-giving Spirit!

And so, by receiving the Eternal Breath of Life (Ruach ha'Kodesh), a person will never be the same. This Third Breath of Yahweh, imparted to humanity as The Set Apart Spirit, is the ultimate and most priceless gift. And it is available to all who believe in and follow Yahshua.

SCRIPTURE REFERENCES:

"And with that he breathed on them and said, '*Receive the Holy Spirit* [Ruach ha'Kodesh].'" (John 20:22, emphasis added)

"Jesus [Yahshua] said to her, 'Everyone who drinks this water will be thirsty again. But whoever drinks the water I give them will never thirst. Indeed, the water I give them will become in them a spring of water welling up to eternal life.'" (John 4:14 NIV)

"On the day of Pentecost all the believers were meeting together in one place. Suddenly, there was a sound from heaven like the roaring of a mighty windstorm, and it filled the house where they were sitting. Then, what looked like flames or tongues of fire appeared and settled on each of them. And everyone present was filled with the Holy Spirit [Ruach ha'Kodesh] and began speaking in other languages, as the Holy Spirit gave them this ability. At that time there were devout Jews from every nation living in Jerusalem. When they heard the loud noise, everyone came running, and they were bewildered to hear their own languages being spoken by the believers. They were completely amazed. 'How can this be?' they exclaimed. 'These people are all from Galilee, and yet we hear them speaking in our own native languages! Here we are—Parthians, Medes, Elamites, people from Mesopotamia, Judea, Cappadocia, Pontus, the province of Asia, Phrygia, Pamphylia, Egypt, and the areas of Libya around Cyrene, visitors from Rome (both Jews and converts to Judaism), Cretans, and Arabs. And we all hear these people speaking in our own languages about the wonderful things God has done!' They stood there amazed and perplexed. 'What can this mean?' they asked each other. But others in the crowd ridiculed them, saying, 'They're just drunk, that's all!' Then Peter stepped forward with the eleven other apostles and shouted to the crowd, 'Listen carefully, all of you, fellow Jews and residents of Jerusalem! Make no mistake about this. These people are not drunk, as some of you are assuming. Nine o'clock in the morning is much too early for that. No, what you see was predicted long ago by the prophet Joel:

"In the last days," God says,
　"I will pour out my Spirit upon all people.
Your sons and daughters will prophesy.
　Your young men will see visions,
　and your old men will dream dreams.
In those days I will pour out my Spirit
　even on my servants—men and women alike—
　and they will prophesy.
And I will cause wonders in the heavens above
　and signs on the earth below—
　blood and fire and clouds of smoke.
The sun will become dark,
　and the moon will turn blood red
　before that great and glorious day of the Lord arrives.
But everyone who calls on the name of the Lord
　will be saved.'" (Acts 2:1–21 NLT)

CHAPTER 7

THE YAHWEH-BREATHED SCRIPTURE

*"All Scripture is **breathed out by God** and profitable for teaching, for reproof, for correction, and for training in righteousness."*

— 2 Timothy 3:16 ESV, emphasis added

In the creation story of Genesis, the stars and vast array of the heavens were made by the Breath of Ruach Elohim, which is the wind or Spirit of Ruach ha'Kodesh (The Holy Spirit). So when Yahweh, Yahshua, and Ruach ha'Kodesh breathe, we can be sure that incredible things happen. We bear witness to Their creativity every time They breathe, because creativity is one of Their defining characteristics. In addition to creative power, when Ruach Elohim breathes, there is an impartation of God's likeness and character.

Don't you want to experience that creative life force in your daily life? One of the gifts of God to humanity is His Word, the Holy Bible. It's an incredible thing that words on a page can be overflowing with life. The same Potter that squeezed life into Adam in the Garden of Eden has squeezed His life force into the very Word of God.

The Breath of Ruach Elohim returns in Paul's letter to Timothy. In this letter, Paul declares that ALL Scripture is God-breathed because Yahweh has imparted attributes of Himself into the Word. It is the life force of Yahweh embedded in the Word that makes it profitable for teaching and rebuking and disciplining and training the hearer in righteousness. Paul further recognizes that the words of men mean nothing (I'm talking about the man or woman or child that does not have Ruach ha'Kodesh living inside), but the words of Yahweh and Ruach Elohim are filled with Their nature.

Consider the underlying message of the verse, "All Scripture is *breathed out by God* and profitable for teaching, for reproof, for correction, and for training in righteousness" (2 Tim. 3:16 ESV, emphasis added). If God has breathed Scripture out (exhaled), then man is responsible for breathing it in (inhaling)! This is another throwback to the moment that automated humanity's breath. In the Garden of Eden, Yahweh breathed out, but there was another response needed from the vessel the Potter had made: Adam had to breathe Him in!

Humanity does not require a breathing tube to be forced down or an emergency medical procedure be undertaken to give breath. Humanity has the gift of the Word of God available to us, and the availability of the Word of God has never been greater, because of the number of Bibles in print, new applications and digital devices to hold it, and more missionaries representing a vast network of distributors like never before. While there are nations where the Word of God itself remains restricted or illegal, still the Word of God is distributed in those nations and finding a way into the hands and hearts of people around the world. Someone, somewhere, who has experienced the Breath of Yahweh will bring His Word to them.

Every year I lead a team of people to small villages in Tanzania. I can personally speak to you about the desperate hunger of men, women, and even young children for the Word of God! And without a doubt the greatest hunger we've seen for God's Word has been among Muslims. They want the Breath of Life! You can only breathe the air in our present atmosphere so long before the desperation for true life and oxygen begins to rise and rise and rise inside of you. No matter what affiliation, background, or story a person has, every living soul needs breath. The Word of God imparts Yahweh's breath. Next time you open the Scripture, take to heart that the life force of Ruach Elohim is in the Word. Not only is it food or daily bread, it is oxygen, a breath from Yahweh into your spiritual being.

Sometimes when I read my Bible, the words on the page suddenly come alive in my heart and I receive encouragement and understanding or revelation about Yahweh, or make a connection I've never made before. Sometimes the words literally correct or discipline me and lead me to repentance and a deeper awareness of the holiness of Yahweh. Sometimes the Word inspires creativity or leads me on a treasure hunt that ends with the discovery of a creative solution. In the case of this book, Yahweh's Word has taken me on a journey that is continually unfolding. First into a sermon, then a book, and now a documentary series and other creative expressions. The Word is alive!

For example, one day I read the Parable of the Ten Minas from Luke. It's definitely a parable from Jesus that makes a person think (Luke 19:11–27). When I read the parable recently (which I've read several times before), I was first of all intrigued and curious about it more than normal. What I mean is I was engaged by the story more than I can remember with previous readings. This time I felt more engagement, I was drawn into the story and wanted to understand it better. Try not to over-spiritualize this moment of reading the Scripture if you can with me. I did not get any clear manifestation in my body while I read this, and no single revelation came to me immediately. But I grew more curious still while I sat there thinking about the meaning of it. In my curiosity I read the passage again. I also read the Parable of the Talents from Matthew because they are such similar parables with similar themes. At this point I felt some understanding about the parables from a practical standpoint. I could see in Yahshua's two stories that there is a master with unlimited wealth and authority who distributes the talents of his kingdom in the way he sees fit. There is a period of time where the recipients of these talents have a personal responsibility to steward them by sowing and reaping and working with what the master has given to each of them. I noted also that not everyone receives the same gifting or authority. Along with some other thoughts, I closed my Bible and went on with my day.

I will pause to reflect here before revealing the next part of this story in God's Word. The understanding I received by reading the two parables was already so practical and life-giving. The revelation of God's Kingdom and the relationship that the parables tell us to have with our Master, Yahweh, are life-changing in themselves. Perhaps these two simple parables, if taken to heart by the many readers of them, have led millions of people to steward what they've been given and honour Yahweh by taking care of (and bearing fruit through) their gifts, abilities, and resources. Imagine an entire world of faithful stewards!

We'd see creativity and God's Kingdom coming in every area of life. The world would become like the Garden of Eden once again. The practical applications in God's Word, and how much clarity and purpose we find within, reveal that the Word is "God-breathed."

But for me, my story with the Parable of the Ten Minas continues. Soon after my curiosity was peaked by this passage, I had a dream. In it I met Joseph, as in the Joseph that was sold by his brothers into slavery in the book of Genesis. Yahweh later raised him to the second in command in the dynasty of Egypt, which was the most powerful nation in the world at the time. In my dream Joseph the patriarch was on a foundation that he had built. He was dressed in modern clothing, steel-toe boots, a modern tool belt. He put down the hammer he was using to make the foundation he stood upon. From within his tool belt he began to take out gold coins, talents, or "minas." He began throwing them to me one after the other. I was standing below the foundation catching the coins, deliberately counting them one at a time and putting them in my own pockets. Twenty-one talents in all.

I won't get into all the details or personal meaning this dream had for me. But mainly the dream was a confirmation of the number of talents my Master has apportioned for me, as indicated by the number of talents in the dream, and also an encouraging visualization of the multiplication that would come from stewarding them. Since our own financial outlook was unstable when I had the dream, I was also greatly encouraged by the dream and reminded that the Kingdom of God is not worldly things, but righteousness, peace, and joy in The Holy Spirit (Rom. 14:17)! The dream was an extension of Ruach ha'Kodesh breathing life on me after life was first breathed, extended, gifted through Yahweh's Word. The meaning of the dream would not have been the same had I not been reading (and drawn more deeply into) the Parable of the Talents at that time.

The Scriptures are filled with Ruach ha'Kodesh and have creative power to change the reader. Furthermore, the Word instructs us to take The Holy Spirit seriously and honour The Set Apart Spirit with our lives. We have been bought at the price of Yahshua's blood, and we are called to honour The Holy Spirit with our every breath.

"Let no unwholesome talk come out of your mouths, but only
what is helpful for building up the one in need and bringing
grace to those who listen. And do not grieve the Holy Spirit of
God, in whom you were sealed for the day of redemption. Get
rid of all bitterness, rage and anger, outcry and slander, along
with every form of malice." (Eph. 4:29–31 BSB)

It's time to walk as one body, breathing in Yahweh's Kingdom by the power of
The Holy Spirit. There is no longer any place in the saved believer for tolerating
the spirit of this age or the breath of the prince of the power of the air in the
world's atmosphere. There are areas that we can walk in greater purity and where
we will honour Ruach ha'Kodesh with our lives by doing so.

First, our actions need to be living signs of Yahweh. This can become a
heated theological debate for some; after all, it's by faith that we are saved, not
by works. But that doesn't foreclose us from doing good works. It's quite the
opposite. The point I want to focus on is that while faith indeed saves, as James so
eloquently put it, "faith without works is dead."

"But someone will say, 'You have faith, and I have works.' Show
me your faith without your works, and I will show you my faith
by my works." (James 2:14 NIV)

I don't know about you, but I'd rather have a living faith than a dead faith.
The works we do are evidence of our faith, not the saving power itself. The other
thing we don't want is to see people doing good works without love, which Paul
said "gains you nothing."

"If I give all I possess to the poor and give over my body
to hardship that I may boast, but do not have love, I gain
nothing." (1 Cor. 13:3 NIV)

The believers that I look up to and try to emulate are the ones who actively
live their faith every day, and they do it out of love. I have a friend who picked up

a homeless man on his way to work one day. After learning about that person's life, they housed him for a season, putting him up for several months in a hotel while he applied for work to find a new job that would allow him to support his own livelihood. When my friend could no longer afford to help this man on his own, he shared the story with a friend, who covered the next month's rent. Another friend of mine has on occasion bought a struggling single parent's groceries at the checkout line. There are many outstanding examples of believers who spend themselves for the benefit of a person in their family or even perfect strangers, serving up love along with their "good works." I love when believers actually share about Yahshua (Jesus) when they do good things for others. I love when believers encourage and uplift the people they do good works for and let them know the Person that lives in them is the reason why they do it. The Holy Spirit bears witness to these kinds of works.

> "For we must all appear before the judgment seat of Christ, so
> that each of us may receive what is due us for the things done
> while in the body, whether good or bad." (2 Cor. 5:10 NIV)

Beyond our actions, our words should be living proof of Yahshua, the Word, being in our lives. Ephesians 4 speaks about this, saying that no unwholesome talk should come from our mouths. Jesus spoke about this powerfully as well by saying in Matthew 12:34 (BSB), "Out of the overflow of the heart the mouth speaks." Jesus refers to the heart in the Greek (which is how the New Testament was written) using the word *kardias*, which also means "the centre of a person, considered to be a reference to the spirit of a person."[14] The heart and spirit are therefore believed by many to abide together. Our words will literally, according to the words of Yahshua, be evidence of our relationship with Jesus. Think about that the next time you're offended by another person's words or if you offend someone with your words. The mouth, in the original Greek text is the word

---

14 Bible Study Tools, s.v. "kardia," accessed May 8, 2020, https://www.biblestudytools.com/lexicons/greek/nas/kardia.html

stoma, which also means "the point of a sword."[15] It was James, one of Jesus' apostles, who said, "Life and death are in the power of the tongue." The tongue is indeed a double-edged sword, able to pierce both the hearer and the speaker. The sword can likewise work in harmony with the Word of God, which makes it a sword that divides bone and marrow, separating flesh from spirit. In the same way, a mouth speaking with the Spirit of Yahshua can sever lies and fears and even break the power of death off a person, bringing healing and life.

Hebrews 4:12 (NIV) says, "For the word of God is alive and active. Sharper than any double-edged sword, it penetrates even to dividing soul and spirit, joints and marrow; it judges the thoughts and attitudes of the heart."

I'll never forget a moment I shared with a young child in Tanzania. We were sitting in a very hot school classroom with a translator, a teacher, and a couple of other young students. I was responsible for sharing some letters and gifts with this young girl that had been sent to her by a sponsor in Canada. There were school supplies, a uniform, and other practical items being given as well as some food for her to take home. As I was communicating through our translator, I could see that this girl was quite distracted. Soon the child was looking blankly at the wall until her face became totally despondent. The translator seemed to be getting a bit uneasy as the "conversation" continued. I could tell something spiritual was going on.

There did not appear to be any physical ailments or health reasons for this behavior, just something in the air that was changing the mood and tone of the classroom. In that moment, I used the sword of my mouth to break through the atmosphere. It was an incredible example of the power of the tongue. Every moment up until that point was being translated from English into Swahili. This child only spoke Swahili. I asked the translator to stop translating for a moment. I declared over that young child some simple truths in my own language, something like, "You are made in the image of God. You are loved by the Creator of the universe. There is nothing that can separate you from the love of God in Christ Jesus."

---

15 Bible Study Tools, s.v. "stoma," accessed May 8, 2020, https://www.biblestudytools.com/lexicons/greek/kjv/stoma.html

All of a sudden the face of this child changed. I mean, the demeanour of this young girl shifted in that instant. Furthermore, the atmosphere and mood inside the classroom shifted as well. We were suddenly able to connect, smile, share conversation. We had an awesome time communicating through our translator after that. The child later joined our team and about a hundred other school children in playing games as well as our creative arts camp outside the classroom. She participated in good spirits and good health.

The Word of God (the revealed power of Ruach ha'Kodesh) transcends language. You can speak His Word with the sword of your mouth as surely as you breathe. The Spirit is on your words when you declare Yahweh's Word.

Revelation 19:15 (NIV) shows the resurrected Yahshua with the sword of His Word: "Coming out of his mouth is a sharp sword with which to strike down the nations. 'He will rule them with an iron scepter.' He treads the winepress of the fury of the wrath of God Almighty."

These images highlight the power of Jesus as the Word of God, and in a micro-sense, they point to the power of our words. We can sprinkle The Set Apart Spirit into our speech and declare God's Word over others.

Practically, we can find truth in God's Word and memorize or read it until we feel able to grasp its significance and meaning. Don't punish yourself if your memorization skills are lacking, because memorization is a good skill to have but definitely not essential. Ruach ha'Kodesh will bring the Word of God to mind for you when you need it or have an opportunity to apply it. At that point you can practice sharing or declaring it to your family, friends, or coworkers.

Another practical application of using God's Word to impact your loved ones is to tell them the life-giving things you see in them. Take a passage of God's Word and apply it to their life, or encourage and build up a coworker or employee in the same way. Speak over your children, literally declaring passages of Scripture over their lives. You can do this when they are awake or even while they are asleep. Take a close friend out for coffee and tell them what they mean to you, but frame it in the truth of Yahweh's Word. You will see the power of your words (which are filled with Yahweh's Word) written all over their faces. You will see the force with which the sword of your mouth impacts your loved ones.

A more difficult practical test: Speak life from God's Word over the people you have a hard time with or even those you consider to be your enemies. Make absolutely sure that you humble yourself and speak from a place of actual love, remembering Yahshua forgave you and saved you while you were still a sinner.

A real-life scenario I faced was with a person I had been having a very hard time with. I chose to spend time practicing what I'm now preaching by meeting this person for lunch at a cafe. In that meeting I purposed to not be defensive or angry with any of the things that were said about me, no matter what they might be. Easier said than done, I assure you. I was aware that they may be tempted to use the sword of their mouth to speak negativity and be hurtful, but what I had control over was my own words. I decided I would practice loving this person by speaking life and kindness through my words, hard as that might be. In this particular meeting, the other person was not clearly changed in their beliefs or position during the course of our lunch. However, the negative tone of their conversation became significantly less forceful and actually dialed down to near-normal levels by the end of our conversation. It didn't take long for the spirit in the air to realize that I would not be baited into a fight. That's what the spirit in the air wants—a swashbuckling clash of words and attitudes dividing the hearts of people.

Meanwhile, the Word of God has dividing power as well, but His Word divides soul and spirit, joints and marrow (Heb. 4:12). The power of this division is that Ruach ha'Kodesh can infill us if we let the new creation breath of Yahweh's Spirit into the deep places of our being!

Here is an interesting fact from *Young Men's Health*: "Do you know that learning to manage anger is good for your health? People who manage their anger get sick less often, and feel better emotionally. Even though anger is a natural emotion sometimes, it can lead to behavior that is uncomfortable or out of control. It may even feel like the anger is controlling you."[16]

Does the part about control sound like evidence of a controlling spirit that has power in the air? How about this physiological nugget from a medical doctor:

---

16 "Anger Management," Young Men's Health, updated July 30, 2019, https://youngmenshealthsite.org/guides/anger-management/

"When a person is stressed or angry, they breathe faster (more shallow breaths). As this persists, it can feel like you are unable to catch your breath."[17]

Your pattern of breathing changes into a more shallow, faster rhythm under stress, anger, fear, negative emotion, or any circumstances that your body determines to be an emergency. From a mental health doctor, "During an emergency, our breathing rate and pattern change. Instead of breathing slowly from our lower lungs, we begin to breathe rapidly and shallowly from our upper lungs. If during this time we are not physically exerting ourselves, then it can produce a phenomenon called 'hyperventilation.' This in turn can explain many of the uncomfortable symptoms during panic, like dizziness, shortness of breath, nausea and confusion. **The good news is that by changing your breathing you can reverse these symptoms."**[18]

The doctors agree: Changing your breathing can reverse the symptoms of panic and anxiety! What grace from Yahweh! You let the peace of God enter your physical body by calmly declaring through your breath, "Yah . . . Weh, Yah . . . Weh." Regardless of race or religion, gender or background, it's a universal grace from God. It's a tremendous, practical truth that can help you through stressful relationships and situations in life.

When I feel my natural heart rate increase in a time of stress, I am working to become consciously aware of my breathing so that I become aware of the truth that Yahweh is on my very breath! The Prince of Peace overcomes the prince of the power of the air.

Our battle has already been won by the Spirit of God, who is already victorious. We don't need to win a war of words with our neighbors; we can operate in a different Spirit than the spirit in the air. What my meeting with the person I had a conflict with did for me was incredible. I left that meeting feeling completely released from any feelings of anger or doubt or unforgiveness toward this person. I actually overcame anxiety over that relationship. I was totally

---

17 "What Does Shortness of Breath Feel Like?" Healthline, updated April 29, 2020, https://www.healthline.com/health/what-does-shortness-of-breath-feel-like

18 "Breathing Problems During Anxiety, and How to Fix Them," Anxieties.com, accessed May 8, 2020, https://www.anxieties.com/57/panic-step4

at peace with God and with that person in my own heart. Every one of us has someone in our life we can practice forgiveness with and use the sword of our mouth to speak life in the name of Yahshua.

I'm not talking about correcting the people in your life. I'm talking about building them up in the gifts and strengths that you see at work in them by the power of The Holy Spirit. Ruach ha'Kodesh is the One who will change them from the inside out. Even if the response you get from the person you share with doesn't satisfy you, it will do something to your own heart, spirit, and attitude. You will feel the power of Yahshua's Word bearing fruit in your life. You might even lead someone to Jesus.

CHAPTER 8

EZEKIEL AND THE DRY BONES

*"Then as I watched, muscles and flesh formed over the bones.
Then skin formed to cover their bodies,
but they still had no breath in them."*

— Ezekiel 37:8 NLT, emphasis added

A young prophet named Ezekiel is walking by a field of wheat on a clear, sunny day. A light breeze makes the heads of wheat sway calmly. The chatter from a small flock of sparrows can be heard in the otherwise quiet field. Suddenly, the calm atmosphere is overtaken by a strong wind that causes the stalks of wheat to bend until they're lying nearly flat upon the soil. Enormous power is in the wind, and Ezekiel struggles to keep both his feet on the ground. The birds have flown away carried by the wind at a fierce pace, narrowly soaring by Ezekiel's face. Now the whirlwind becomes a funnel cloud, and Ezekiel is swept inside the cloud. Ten feet in the air, now twenty, a hundred. Around him the chaos continues, but inside the cloud the power of the wind is suddenly calm. Once simply afraid, now a reverent awe comes over Ezekiel. He suddenly realizes he is not in a cloud at all. He is inside the very presence of Yahweh.

The Spirit of Yahweh carries the prophet a great distance before setting him down in a desolate valley. Coming closer to the earth, the red soil gives way to what look like bones—millions of bones. The entire valley is full of skeletons. When Yahweh puts Ezekiel down, the breeze shifts, filling his nostrils with the unmistakable stench of death. Dry bones, decaying bodies, and death riddle the valley as far as the eye can see. An ominous post-apocalyptic sight.

Yahweh turns toward the prophet and asks, "Son of man, can these bones live?" Ezekiel surveys the expanse before him, shrugs his shoulders, and replies, "Sovereign Yahweh, You alone know." Then Yahweh says to him, "Prophesy to these bones and say to them, 'Dry bones, hear the word of the Lord [Yahweh]! This is what the Sovereign Lord [Yahweh] says to these bones: I will make breath [ruach] enter you, and you will come to life. I will attach tendons to you and make flesh come upon you and cover you with skin; I will put breath in you, and you will come to life. Then you will know that I am the Lord [Yahweh]'" (Ezekiel 37:3–6 NIV).

Ezekiel prophesies as commanded. As he is prophesying, there is a noise, a rattling sound, and the bones come together, bone to bone. Ezekiel looks, and tendons and flesh appear on the bones and skin covers them. *But there is no breath in them.*

Then Yahweh says, "Prophesy to the breath; prophesy, son of man, and say to it, 'This is what the Sovereign Lord [Yahweh] says: Come, breath, from the four winds and breathe into these slain, that they may live.' So I prophesied as he commanded me, *and breath entered them*; they came to life and stood up on their feet—a vast army." (Ezekiel 37:9–10 NIV)

Like Ezekiel, what we see in humanity is that when we become disconnected from our Creator Yahweh, the source of our life, we begin to break down and decay. Moral decay and sin lead to death both physically and spiritually.

The choice of Adam and Eve to disobey Yahweh in the Garden of Eden represented a spiritual death instantly, while their physical death sentence was also triggered because of sin. The consequences of sin were extreme because the relationship between Creator and His creation was broken. The Billy Graham Evangelistic Association puts it this way: "As soon as Adam sinned, man was separated from God and death began. It was as if a spiritual virus was placed in the DNA of humanity forever. Although God created us in His image to have abundant life and fellowship with Him, the image was marred and the fellowship was shattered. The entire human race went from innocence to sinfulness in one fell swoop."[19]

I believe the neshawmaw breath of life that Adam and Eve lived from before they ate of the tree of the knowledge of good and evil was different. Before sin, the breath of life was pure, it was received from Yahweh and breathed back to Him with every single breath. The dependence of humanity on God was tied to that breath, and there was no disconnect in understanding that Yahweh was their oxygen and the source of their very life.

Sin came through the first Adam, and although humanity continually inherits the DNA of sin and separation from Yahweh because of sin, through Yahshua (Jesus) there is now a new breath of life available to every dead or dying person in the world.

This truth is powerfully depicted in the Book of Ezekiel. I believe it is a Scripture with obvious truth for Ezekiel's time, for our time, and for the future. It also reveals the heart of Yahweh, which is to empower humanity to operate in partnership with the life-giving Spirit of Ruach ha'Kodesh.

Not surprisingly, the secret unveiled to Ezekiel is all about breath (Ezek. 37:1–10).

Ezekiel's famous prophecy about the valley of dry bones is all about the ruach (breath/spirit) of life from Yahweh. Ezekiel's encounter was as significant for the ancient people of Israel as it is for the Body of Christ today. The picture of resurrection points to the power of Ruach ha'Kodesh and the quickening power of the Spirit to bring the dead to life. Yahweh even says, "I will put breath in you so that you come to life. *Then* you will know that I am Yahweh." (Ezekiel 37:6 WEB, emphasis added)

The proof that Yahweh is the Breath of Life is evidenced by Yahweh's Ruach (Spirit) bringing something that was dead to life.

It's very similar to the moment of creation in the Garden of Eden. Remember how Yahweh formed the first Adam in the Garden of Eden? Although flesh was on the bone, Adam was still not alive. So it was with Ezekiel. He prophesied to

---

19 Skip Heitzig, "Step Two: Separation From God," Decision magazine, September 23, 2004, https://decisionmagazine.com/step-two-separation-from-god/

the bones, and they came together like Adam in the garden: bone came to bone and then tendons and flesh appeared and finally skin covered all of the bodies.

Ezekiel 37:8b (NIV), "But there was no breath in them."

The same picture that Yahweh Himself saw in the garden emerges for Ezekiel. I wonder whether the Father, Son, or Holy Spirit asked the question at that time, the moment before They breathed on Adam, "Can these dry bones live?"

And then Yahweh prophesied to Adam by breathing, "Y-H-W-H, YOD-HEY-WAW- HEY," the sound of breath, the sound of His name over Adam, and Adam (the sculpture formerly known as dirt and dry bones) came alive!

What's fascinating about the short form of His name, "I AM," is that it can be translated as "He Will Be." I'm still trying to fathom the full significance of this: Every breath has been infused with power to create. The spirit or attitude in which we breathe will either create life or death. The macro truth behind this is that whatever we declare or pray or speak or breathe "will come to be."

Ruach Elohim teaches Ezekiel how to bring His life-giving Spirit into the dead bones. He says prophesy to the breath (spirit) and say to it, "Come, breath [ruach], from the four winds and breathe into these slain, that they may live." (Ezekiel 37:9 NIV)

What a profound picture of co-laboring with Yahweh. Ezekiel, who represents humanity in the prophecy, is called to hear from the LORD (Yahweh) and then declare His word prophetically (in the Spirit) to change the atmosphere physically. He's literally taught how to breathe life.

And who else does the Scripture point to? Ezekiel himself is referred to as "son of man" in the passage; in fact, he's called that over ninety times throughout the Book of Ezekiel. This label is symbolic because Ezekiel represents the coming Messiah in the prophetic imagery, as this is the same term that Yahshua repeatedly used in the New Testament during His life on earth: Son of Man.

The Son of Man, Yahshua (Yahweh Who Saves), operated as a human being on earth and performed miracles as mighty as Ezekiel performed when he prophesied to the breath (spirit) of the bones. One of the miracles the Messiah would have to do, according to Jewish belief, in order to prove that He was in fact Messiah was raise someone from the dead. Three resurrections are recorded during Yahshua's ministry, including a young man in a funeral procession on the way to his burial (Luke 7:11–17), a young daughter of a synagogue leader who had just died in her bed (Luke 8:49–56) and Lazarus, who had been dead inside a tomb for four days (John 11:1–44).

There are ten recorded resurrection scenes in the Bible that appear throughout the Old and New Testament. Most intriguingly, on three separate occasions—once with the Prophet Elijah, once with the Prophet Elisha, and once with the Apostle Paul—the dead are raised back to life when the healer lies on top of them and places his mouth over the dead person's mouth!

They bring them back through the power of Yahweh and their breath.

Since I received the word *breath* from Ruach ha'Kodesh and started digging into the narrative in Scripture around breath, I've become much more aware of the power of The Holy Spirit to change my circumstances and influence for His glory the ones I love and the people I meet. I can see that my words (and my mouth itself) are a sword and that I can wield and speak words filled with The Set Apart Spirit. I can prophesy breath (spirit) over the broken bones, lifeless people, and dead or dying things around me. I can choose to inhale Yahweh's Spirit from inside of me, letting flow rivers of living water.

I've also witnessed how the name of Yahweh transcends language and culture. I've seen the effectiveness of Ruach ha'Kodesh at work in my life in Canada as well as Thailand, Cambodia, Tanzania, India, and other places I've been.

I don't know exactly where the dead bones are in your life. Your relationships. Your marriage. Your children. Your faith might seem dead. Your finances might seem dead. Something in your world, as long as we are part of the present age, is either dying or completely void of life. But like Ezekiel and the many millions that came before us and witnessed the same valley of death lying desolately before them, the question remains, "Can these dry bones live?"

As surely as Yahweh lives, yes, these dry bones can live, and they will be made alive by the power of Ruach ha'Kodesh, The Set Apart Holy Spirit, the life-giving force of Yahweh's Breath!

Practice this today: Breathe life over your circumstances. *Breathe* (speak, whisper, emote) *life* (the life-giving Spirit of Ruach ha'Kodesh) *over your circumstances* (hover over the waters of your circumstances in prayer and begin to ask Yahweh for creativity).

It's worth repeating an abbreviated version of the practical exercise shared earlier in this book. To perform this exercise, begin by finding a quiet place where you will not be distracted—no phones or immediate interruptions. You can read the four steps as an overview of the exercise, then come back to step one and try it yourself.

Step one: Begin to breathe deeply, relax, and imagine that right now you are alone with Ruach Elohim (Yahweh, Yahshua, Ruach ha'Kodesh—the Father, Son, and Holy Spirit). Become aware of the circumstance that you want to breathe life over.

Step two: Breathe in and imagine that you are not inhaling air, you are inhaling Ruach ha'Kodesh, The Set Apart Spirit.

Step three: Before you exhale, pause to imagine The Holy Spirit indwelling your whole person. You're holding in the Holy Breath of Life, letting it infill your body, soul, and spirit.

Step four: Exhale, with faith or belief that you are breathing out the very Spirit of God upon the circumstance or relationship you are praying about.

Repeat the process as you move through the prayer requests or circumstances that are on your heart. Repeat the process again as a way of communing with The Holy Spirit. As you continue this process, remember that it is not a religious process that requires you do it in the same way or become fixated on the steps. This is not about religion. This is simply a strategy to help you become more aware that Yahweh is your Breath of Life.

I want to be a co-laborer with Yahweh in breathing new creation life into the circumstances and situations that are dead or simply need an infusion of resurrection life! I want to see The Set Apart Spirit of Yahweh bring to life or bring a more Spirit-filled life to my family, my friends, my church, my business endeavors, and everything else in my life.

I am simply sharing one personal strategy that amazes me. By praying like this, I hope that you will experience The Holy Spirit stirring in you, dancing within you, whispering to you.

If you need to operate with a little more intensity, feel free to turn on worship music (or any music that helps you focus on Yahweh). Begin to sing or speak or whisper quietly over your circumstances. Let your heart begin to believe with certainty that the dead bones you are facing WILL LIVE. Declare the truth over your situation until you begin to see the dead body of your situation breathing with life again.

You will see new life come when you declare the name of Yahweh over your circumstances. Practice breathing His holy name over the dry bones that you face. Then watch the power of Yahweh go to work.

CHAPTER 9

THE CROWN OF HIS CREATION

A promise great enough to live your life for is this: If you confess Yahshua's name before men, He will confess your name before Yahweh in Heaven. In other words, if you breathe in Ruach ha'Kodesh, The Set Apart Spirit, and as surely as you breathe, your own spirit is sanctified, Yahshua will breathe your name back to Yahweh. Your spirit will be saved by the power of His breath.

> "Therefore whoever confesses Me before men, him I will also confess before My Father who is in heaven." (Matt. 10:32 NKJV)

I'll give one example of confessing Yahshua's name "before men." We've known a sweet woman in Thailand since my wife, Christy, and her dad went there in 2006. Our family has revisited her three or four times on different visits to Thailand. The first time we met her, she had a restaurant, a home, and a family. When I met her again in 2019, she was sleeping on a cold concrete floor in a factory, had lost her house, lost her closest family members to premature death, and tragically her niece had just been taken from her by a government agency. With the loss of her home and a large debt to pay, she faced possible jail time in a Thai prison.

While we spent time with her, I felt a strong prompting from The Holy Spirit to read Isaiah 61 out loud, quoting the verses while looking into her eyes. There have been few moments in my life where a Scripture has been more pertinent in every nuance of the verses. After the Lord gave Isaiah 61 to our team as a theme verse for the trip, I was unaware that we would be crossing paths with this woman. It was not supposed to be part of our itinerary. I had no idea what type of problems she was facing. But as we laid hands on this sixty-five-year-old woman, I looked into her eyes quoting Isaiah 61 while tears streamed down her face.

"Good news to the poor."

"The oil of Joy instead of a spirit of despair."

"I the Lord [Yahweh] love Justice, I hate robbery and wrongdoing."

Because we have a Kingdom bestowed on us if we follow Yahshua and are filled with Ruach ha'Kodesh, we have to see ourselves, in these moments, as the very hands and feet and breath of Yahweh. Honestly, there was more than one voice in the atmosphere saying things like, "Maybe she isn't telling the truth. Maybe she isn't really in as much trouble as she says. She's a liar. Can she really be trusted?"

But rather than getting sideswiped by the doubts all around us in the air, what if we tried living out the Way, the Truth, and the Spirit of Life? Why not see where that takes us? Why not see what breathing Ruach ha'Kodesh does for the ones around us who are trapped in the kingdom of darkness? Breathing life in this instance meant sharing The Holy Spirit through our actions of love, giving, relationship building, paying off debts, and connecting her with friends at a local church.

Generally, breathing the Spirit of Life means following whatever specific instructions are given by The Holy Spirit for the circumstances you find yourself in. Remember that Ruach Elohim operates with a spirit of great creativity. The actions and words required will almost certainly vary from case to case and day to day.

Our friend from Thailand recently messaged me, "I am going to find a church to learn more about Jesus." This is everything. A moment of bestowing God's Kingdom can lead a person on a journey to finding their everlasting crown if we direct them to the name of Yahshua when we do it.

> "And God [Yahweh] is able to *bestow* every blessing on you in abundance, so that richly enjoying all sufficiency at all times, you may have ample means for all good works." (2 Cor. 9:8 WNT, emphasis added)

He bestows His Kingdom on His followers so that we are empowered to do good works and bring others into a shared and glorious inheritance! But to accept the glory God has bestowed on us, we have to recognize that He is glorious.

I want to point one last time to the example from the beginning of this book, which reminds me how big Yahweh is. An astrophysicist described that recently Hubble Telescope had been pointing for days into an empty black patch of nothingness. Then they appeared! Hundreds of billions of never-before-seen galaxies! The most straightforward estimate using today's best technology points to there being one hundred seventy billion galaxies in our universe. But the modern estimate is far grander: two trillion galaxies. Inside a typical galaxy, like our Milky Way, is an estimated one hundred billion stars. The conclusion was that there are more stars in the universe than all the grains of sand on all of Earth's ocean beaches.

The grandiose awesomeness of Yahweh, Yahshua, and Ruach ha'Kodesh will continue to fascinate our imaginations and fill our spirits with life and wonder for all of eternity.

I love the relationship of the Trinity of God in the creation story. In the narrative, we meet God (Ruach Elohim is plural, not singular) in three Persons, in fact, the Father, Son, and Holy Spirit are all clearly represented in the Genesis narrative.

The Father, Yahweh, is speaking the words, and Yahshua is the Word, the manifestation of the invisible God in the flesh. The Apostle Paul speaks about this in Colossians, and the Apostle John opens his Gospel with a poignant parallel to Genesis 1:1.

> "In the beginning was the Word, and the Word was with God,
> and the Word was God. He was with God in the beginning.
> Through Him all things were made, and without Him nothing
> was made that has been made." (John 1:1–3 BSB)

Clearly, the Father and Son are at work, but The Holy Spirit is at work too. Psalm 33:6 (NKJV, emphasis added) says, "By the word of the LORD [Yahweh] the heavens were made, and all the host of them by the *breath* [ruach] *of His mouth.*"

The host of heaven, which could be referring to the stars, was made by the "breath of His mouth." Through this we learn that the host of Heaven was made by The Holy Spirit or Ruach of the Almighty. This is emphasized again in Job 26:13 (NKJV): "By His Spirit [Ruach] He adorned the heavens."

I stated at the beginning of this book that I only wrote it because God whispered the word *breath* to me. By studying this word in Scripture, my relationship with God has come alive like never before. As a direct result of the whisper of Yahweh, I'm becoming more and more aware that Yahweh is literally my Breath of Life.

I want to invite you back into the Garden of Eden once again.

It's no longer Adam that Yahweh is cradling with a loving hand—it's you. The earth and the heavens and the vast universe and the animals and trees and flowers have already been spoken into existence. They've heeded the Word of God and come to be. And now Ruach Elohim has entered Earth's atmosphere from a hovering vantage point, landing in the intimacy of a garden.

While you breathe in the aroma of a million fresh flowers, He is there in the midst of it all. The Beginning and the End. The Alpha and the Omega. He has robes concealing His radiant glory, but His face shines brighter than the sun on a cloudless day. Yahweh walks toward you at the centre of the garden. Yahweh's hand reaches down, touching the earth He created for the first time. He scoops up the best material, pliable yet firm clay soaking up some of the moisture from the stream.

He smiles because He carries a great secret. The earth gives way beneath His hands, which are calloused yet somehow unworn. They have witnessed ages pass by, yet they are still soft and warm, like the tender palm of a young father grasping the hand of his son.

For the first moment in history Yahweh can be seen by the rest of creation in a position of vulnerability, getting His hands dirty in the mud, slime, and dust of the earth. This is your Father and this is God, a masterful sculptor. He begins to form and shape you. Remarkably, you take on His character, His shape . . . though you still feel as though you are only dust.

Until Yahweh, cradling your head with compassion unmatched since the creation of the world, draws you within inches of His face. His glory at this distance is unfathomably bright, and the weight of His presence threatens to pull apart the very cells of your being. An explosion of creativity is about to take place. An explosion of life is about to be imparted. For as He draws you in, He inhales a divine breath, exhaling upon your body, soul, and spirit the sound of His name: YAH . . . WEH!

For while the vast universe was crowned with glory, within the universe YOU ARE THE CROWN of Ruach Elohim's creation!

You have been made in His image; in the image of Yahweh you have been created. When you inhale Yahweh's life force for the first time, you come alive. There are no other life forms in Heaven or on earth that have been made as special as you. No other beings were ever labeled image-bearers of Yahweh, therefore you and I are unique and special and beautiful and immensely creative beings. We bear the image of the Creator of everything! Therefore we are called to be like Him.

God is Spirit. God is love. God is a life-giving, miracle-working, creative artist! We are called to be life-giving, miracle-working, creative artists! We are called to breathe Him in so we can breathe Him out to the world in order that the "crown of His creation" might someday receive an everlasting crown.

The resurrected and reigning Yahshua (Jesus) has bestowed on each of us the Kingdom of Yahweh, and the promises of this future crown.

"In the future there is laid up for me the crown of
righteousness, which the Lord [Yahshua], the righteous Judge,
will award to me on that day; and not only to me, but also to all
who have loved His appearing." (2 Tim. 4:8 NASB)

The appearing of Yahshua is the most beautiful and awesome moment in any believer's life. And if a person will simply love His appearing, they will be given the crown of righteousness. To love His appearing is to confess His name and believe that Yahweh raised Yahshua from the dead.

"Blessed is a man who perseveres under trial; for once he has
been approved, he will receive the crown of life which the Lord
[Yahshua] has promised to those who love Him." (James 1:12
NASB)

James reiterates that if we love the most awe-inspiring One in the universe, we will receive the crown of life! How difficult is He to love? Yahshua set you free for a victorious life when He paid the entire bounty on your head and gave you a sure promise of eternity with Him. There is no one (and nothing) in all creation that is more lovable!

"Be faithful until death, and I will give you the crown of life."
(Rev. 2:10b NKJV)

Have you noticed that the apostles and prophets were unwavering even in the face of death? Stephen, the first martyr, witnessed the throne room of Heaven as he was stoned to death. Paul the apostle sought to get closer and closer to the fires of Rome in order to accelerate his life's ending, having glimpsed the coming glory (2 Cor. 12:2–4). We share a faith that is not threatened by death. Death is a final enemy that has been ultimately defeated through the death and resurrection of Yahshua. Ruach ha'Kodesh has sealed us for the day of redemption, when we will stand before Yahshua and receive an unfading crown of glory.

"And when the Chief Shepherd appears, you will receive the
crown of glory that will never fade away." (1 Pet. 5:4 NIV)

The crown we will receive from Yahshua is invaluable. We will also be
crowned because of what we do here on earth in leading others into the Kingdom
of Yahweh and His Christ. Your crown will be decorated and arrayed in glory
as you disciple, love, and lead others to Yahshua. A day is coming when you
will see the train of people brought into Yahshua's Kingdom through your life
and ministry, and on that glorious day your crown will be adorned with jewels
representing the treasures of Yahweh's kingdom—the people of God. Yahweh
Himself will crown you with a crown of glory that will never tarnish or fade.

"For who is our hope or joy or crown of exultation? Is it not
even you, in the presence of our Lord Jesus [Yahshua] at His
coming? For you are our glory and joy." (1 Thess. 2:19–20
NKJV)

I imagine these moments when I reflect on the wonders of Yahweh's creation,
when I consider the magnitude and scale of Yahshua, the Word of God, making
the universe; when I breathe in the reality of Ruach ha'Kodesh at work, arraying
the heavens and earth with splendor and coming to earth at Pentecost to begin
living inside believers, making the very people He loves into the temple of His
presence. I tremble in awe mixed with joy when I consider what the moment will
be like when all of humanity stands before His presence and the Book of Life is
opened.

Every spirit breathed from the mouth of Yahweh together in one place. All
of history's famous, infamous, and totally unknown. The hidden champions
of our faith alongside the patriarchs and matriarchs of our faith. Every villain,
sinner, and criminal. Children and adults, the rich and poor, small and great.
Nothing else will matter; the desire and fixation of every single breath, every
spirit through the ages, will be to breathe the name of YAHWEH in holiness,
without blaspheming it or taking it in vain. Imagine the unity there will be when
we realize all together that Yahweh is literally all in all. Imagine all humanity

together realizing our very existence relies on the Breath of Life, which is Yahweh's very name. But if you have no sure salvation (the Hebrew word is *Yahshua*), just imagine the trembling in that place.

> "Therefore God has highly exalted him and *bestowed* on him
> the name that is above every name, so that at the name of Jesus
> [Yahshua] every knee should bow, in heaven and on earth and
> under the earth, and every tongue confess that Jesus Christ is
> Lord, to the glory of God the Father [Yahweh]." (Phil. 2:9–11
> ESV, emphasis added)

To be certain that your name will be read before Yahweh from the Lamb's Book of Life, you have to confess and believe in Him. He's the most magnificent wonder in all creation. Believing in Him is simple.

> "If you declare with your mouth, 'Jesus is Lord,' and believe
> in your heart that God raised him from the dead, you will be
> saved." (Rom. 10:9 NIV)

And all together, all who are known to Yahshua will breathe The Set Apart Spirit as one, and we will all be changed. We will become one heart, one body, one spirit. Together we will inhale and exhale our very first YAH . . . WEH, and we will never breathe the same again.

Yod: A divine moment of intention, where all humanity—past, present, and future—pause together, eyes fixed on the throne of the Almighty.

Hey: A holy inhale of the very manifest presence of the Almighty Yahweh, seated on the throne of glory beside Yahshua, the Alpha and Omega, the First and the Last.

Waw: Another pause, the Breath of Life infilling and penetrating every cell of the resurrected body.

Hey: Our first exhale as the Body of Christ, united by the power of Ruach ha'Kodesh.

As you take a few more breaths while reading this book, consider the words of Yahshua from Revelation 3:5–6 (BSB), "Like them, the one who is victorious will be dressed in white. And I will never blot out his name from the book of life, but I will confess his name before My Father [Yahweh] and His angels. He who has an ear, let him hear what the Spirit [Ruach ha'Kodesh] says to the churches."

The Breath of Yahweh, Yahshua, and Ruach ha'Kodesh shape the narrative of humanity. They are the Breath of Life for all who believe. It's time to breathe like you have never breathed before.

AFTERWORD

Do you have The Holy Spirit (Ruach ha'Kodesh)? And are you breathing in and breathing out the Spirit or Breath of Yahweh in your daily life? Because if you breathe in His Breath, you will breathe out the fruit of His Spirit.

This moment is an opportunity for anyone who needs a fresh breath or a first breath of The Holy Spirit to receive the breath of life.

If you want Yahshua (Jesus) to breathe His life over any part of your body or spirit, the activation is just so simple.

Fix your heart for a moment on the face of Yahshua, Jesus your Savior. Fix your heart on the Father Yahweh and on The Holy Spirit (Ruach ha'Kodesh), whose presence is all around you right now.

Begin to breathe in His love and life and inhale His Set Apart Spirit. I invite you to say His holy name, His beautiful, life-giving name, by breathing from a position of worship. Say *Yah-Weh* as you breathe. Say *Yahshua* as you breathe. Say *Ruach ha'Kodesh* as you breathe.

Rather than continuing to breathe your way through life in anger or bitterness or sin, you can choose right now to breathe your way through life with your heart and soul fixed on Yahshua (Jesus), fixed on The Set Apart Spirit of God (Ruach ha'Kodesh), fixed on the Creator of the universe and your loving Father (Yahweh).

I invite you to stay focused on The Holy Spirit and to breathe in the presence of Yahweh's Spirit. Talk with Yahshua in your own words, or pray this simple prayer:

Thank You, Yahshua (Jesus), that You paid the price for my sins and rose from the dead by the power of The Holy Spirit (Ruach ha'Kodesh). Thank You, Yahweh, that You made me in Your image and gave me the breath of life and a spirit. I believe in You, Yahshua, and I ask You to fill me with Your Holy Spirit, Your Set Apart Spirit, the same Spirit that raised Yahshua from the dead. I repent for the sin I have committed against Your Holy Spirit and Holy Name, and I repent for being influenced by the power of the air. I receive You, Yahshua, as Lord of my life, and I invite You, Holy Spirit, Ruach ha'Kodesh, to fill me with Your new life today. I choose You, Yahweh, as my Breath of Life. Amen.

"The Spirit of God has made me, And the breath of the Almighty [Yahweh] gives me life." (Job 33:4 NKJV)

"You send forth Your Spirit [Breath], they are created." (Ps. 104:30 NKJV)

So God, as I breathe today . . . every breath I take, I take in You. *YAH . . . WEH . . .*

APPENDIX

Breath of life, from the root word in Hebrew *neshawmaw*:

> "And the LORD God formed man *of* the dust of the ground, and breathed into his nostrils the breath of life [neshawmaw]; and man became a living soul." (Gen. 2:7 KJV)

Other examples of the use of *neshawmaw* are:

> "All in whose nostrils *was* the breath of life [neshawmaw], of all that *was* in the dry *land*, died." (Gen. 7:22 KJV)

> "All the while my breath [neshawmaw] is in me, and the spirit of God is in my nostrils." (Job 27:3 KJV)

> "The spirit of God hath made me, and the breath [neshawmaw] of the Almighty hath given me life." (Job 33:4 KJV)

> "The spirit of man [neshawmaw] is the candle of the LORD [Yahweh], searching all the inward parts of the belly." (Prov. 20:27 KJV)

> "He that spread forth the earth . . . he that giveth breath [neshawmaw] unto the people upon it, and spirit to them that walk therein." (Isa. 42:5 KJV)

The power of His name:

Not many have a revelation of the power of His name. The apostle John emphasizes the power of His name throughout his Gospel. First, John records Yahshua (Jesus) saying that He came in the Father's name. His Father's name is Yahweh.

> "I have come in My Father's name, and you do not receive Me; if another comes in his own name, him you will receive." (John 5:43 NKJV)

It later says that Jesus performs miracles in the Father's name. His Father's name is Yahweh.

> "Jesus answered them, 'I told you, and you do not believe. The works that I do in My Father's name, they bear witness of Me.'" (John 10:25 NKJV)

Jesus then taught that we can ask anything in *His name* and we will receive it, demonstrating that the Father and Son are one.

> "And whatever you ask in My name, that I will do, that the Father may be glorified in the Son." (John 14:13 NKJV)

He also taught that we are kept safe in Yahweh's name.

> "Now I am no longer in the world, but these are in the world, and I come to You. Holy Father, keep through Your name those whom You have given Me, that they may be one as We *are*." (John 17:11 NKJV)

Scripture references that include the word *bestow*:

The mystery of our faith is that we are recipients of all the gifts of Yahweh that were earned through the blood of Yahshua. The truth of this was already at work before Jesus died two thousand years ago. I want to invite you to read the following Scriptures and while you do, breathe slowly and receive some of the gifts and promises bestowed on you by Yahweh, by Yahshua, by Ruach ha'Kodesh.

> "He lifts the weak from the dust; he raises the poor from the ash heap to seat them with princes—he *bestows* on them an honored position. The foundations of the earth belong to the LORD [Yahweh]—he placed the world on them." (1 Sam. 2:8 NET, emphasis added)

> "How great is your favor, which you store up for your loyal followers! In plain sight of everyone you *bestow* it on those who take shelter in you." (Ps. 31:19 NET, emphasis added)

> "[Jesus said] I *bestow* on you a kingdom, just as My Father *bestowed* one on Me." (Luke 22:29 HCSB, emphasis added)

Note: I discovered that in this verse *bestow* is derived from the Greek in the context of "making a will," as in a last will and testament. What it means is He wrote you into His will, and in His will you inherit His Kingdom! Just as Yahshua (Jesus) inherited it from His Father (Yahweh)—which also means you're in His family, you are His son or daughter, you are His heir, and you rightfully receive His inheritance by the power of Yahweh's Spirit.

> "May the LORD's [Yahweh's] face enlighten you and bestow favor on you." (Num. 6:25 ISV)

"So now in the sight of all Israel, the assembly of Yahweh, and in the hearing of our God, observe and seek all the commandments of Yahweh your God so that you may take possession of this good land and bestow *it* as an inheritance to your children after you forever." (1 Chron. 28:8 LEB)

"O LORD, show us your loyal love. Bestow on us your deliverance." (Ps. 85:7 NET)

"The rod and rebuke bestow wisdom, but an undisciplined child brings shame to his mother." (Prov. 29:15 ISV)

"The nations will see your vindication, and all the kings your glory; and people will call you by a new name that the mouth of the LORD [Yahweh] will bestow." (Isa. 62:2 ISV)

"God exalted Him to His right hand to be Prince *and* Leader and Savior *and* Deliverer *and* Preserver, in order to grant repentance to Israel and to bestow forgiveness *and* release from sins." (Acts 5:31 AMPC)

Scripture references about Yahshua and Ruach ha'Kodesh:

The Scriptures tell us,

"The first man, Adam, became a living person." But the last Adam—that is, Christ—is a life-giving Spirit. What comes first is the natural body, then the spiritual body comes later. Adam, the first man, was made from the dust of the earth, while Christ, the second man, came from heaven. Earthly people are like the earthly man, and heavenly people are like the heavenly man. Just as we are now like the earthly man, we will someday be like the heavenly man. (1 Cor. 15:45-49 NLT)

"For just as the Father raises the dead and gives them life, so also the Son gives life to whom he wishes." (John 5:21 NET)

"Just as the living Father sent Me and I live because of the Father, so also the one who feeds on Me will live because of Me." (John 6:57 HCSB)

"Nevertheless, death reigned from Adam until Moses, even over those who did not sin in the way that Adam transgressed. He is a pattern of the One to come." (Romans 5:14 BSB)

"For in Christ Jesus the law of the Spirit of life has set you free from the law of sin and death." (Rom. 8:2 EHV)

"How much more will the blood of Christ, who through the eternal Spirit offered Himself without blemish to God, purify our consciences from dead works to worship the living God!" (Heb. 9:14 NET)

"What is the immeasurable greatness of his power toward us who believe, according to the working of his great might that he worked in Christ when he raised him from the dead." (Eph. 1:19–20 ESV)